CROSSWAYS

This book is dedicated to
Colleen
My beautiful wife
and forever friend.

CROSSWAYS

Forming Ourselves in the Mind of Christ

When each life is measured
for its pearl of great price,
May the path that I treasured
be the crossways to Christ.

JAMES HOGAN

ALBA·HOUSE   NEW·YORK

SOCIETY OF ST. PAUL, 2187 VICTORY BLVD., STATEN ISLAND, NEW YORK 10314

ST PAULS

Library of Congress Cataloging-in-Publication Data

Hogan, James.
   Crossways: forming ourselvbes in the mind of Christ /
James Hogan.
      p.   cm.
   ISBN 0-8189-0870-X
   1. Christian life — Catholic authors. I. Title.
BX2350.2.H5865   2000
242 — dc21   99-27738
                                    CIP

Produced and designed in the United States of America by the
Fathers and Brothers of the Society of St. Paul,
2187 Victory Boulevard, Staten Island, New York 10314-6603,
as part of their communications apostolate.

ISBN: 0-8189-0870-X

Printing Information:

Current Printing - first digit 1 2 3 4 5 6 7 8 9 10

Year of Current Printing - first year shown

2000   2001   2002   2003   2004   2005   2006   2007   2008

Table of Contents

PART THREE: THE CENTER OF THE CROSS

Acknowledgments

Not only does our Lord work in mysterious ways, He works in numerous ways as well. Many wonderful people have been the instrument of His love in my life. Allow me to thank only a few of them.

I wish to thank my Father and Mother for their gifts of steadfast faith and earnest love. A son could have no better Mom. And as for my Dad, if I become half the father he was to me, I will consider myself richly blessed.

I wish to thank my family for their inspiration: my loving wife Colleen, an Irish rose, for all of her brilliant advice and emotional support on this endeavor; my children Clare, Kate, Erin, and Thomas — four emeralds of laughter and joy whom I will treasure always; my brothers John and Michael; my sisters Maureen and Kathleen; and John and Kay O'Malley who welcomed me into their family as well.

I must express my gratitude to Fr. Edmund Lane, SSP and all the people of Alba House who have believed in me and made this book a reality. They are a real Christian community.

I wish to thank the great teacher, writer, and mentor Dr. Michael Pennock. Any good I have done or will do in teaching and writing, I owe to him.

Particular thanks go to my inspirational department chairman and friend James Skerl, who has taught me what real holiness is, and to my great companion in Christ Tom Becks, who has taught me what true friendship is.

My thanks also go to some of my tremendous friends and colleagues at Saint Ignatius High School who have helped me become a better writer and better person — especially Paul Prokop, Marty Dybicz, the Irish twins Tom Healey and Jim Brennan, Dan Galla, Karl Ertle, Pat Ertle, Fr. Larry Ober, Gail Scaravelli, Joe Ptak, and the wordsmith Joe Toner.

Last, I would like to express my deepest appreciation to my students past and present who have blessed me over the years. It has been an honor teaching men and women of their caliber.

To all of these and all others who have given so much to me over the years, I thank you. God bless you.

A Jesus Prayer

Jesus. You are the *Light* we must see.
Jesus. You are the *Word* we must hear.
Jesus. You are the *Gift* we must give.
Jesus. You are the *Love* we must share.
Jesus. You are the *Joy* we must express.
Jesus. You are the *Key* we must possess.
Jesus. You are the *Way* we must follow.
Jesus. You are the *Truth* we must seek.
Jesus. You are the *Life* we must live.
Jesus. You are the *Friend* we must have.
Jesus. You are the *King* we must serve.
Jesus. You are the *God* we must will.
Amen.

Introduction

Camelot

*"Amen, I say to you, whoever does not accept the king-
dom of God like a little child will not enter it."*
Mark 10:15

I lived in the land of Catholic Camelot. A fortress of Christianity surrounded my childhood — complete with confessionals and
crucifixes, Hail Mary's and holy days, fast-pitch baseball and
fasting. I have wonderful memories of the *kyrie eleison* and pa-
rochial school "daze" spent dreaming about girls. I've often
thought that I spent so much time with my head in the clouds,
that I could have "lettered" in daydreaming in grade school and
placed first in state competition. Like most children, thoughts
of Christ were important though infrequent. Nevertheless, like
an omnipresent perfume, the Christ of faith permeated the air I
breathed. Secure in the faith and love given through my family,
I walked the *crossways* to Christ.

Even the airwaves did not contradict the *crossways*. Like
many Catholic boys, instead of immersing myself in fractions and
phonics, I watched "Speed Racer" and "The Partridge Family."
Needless to say, this did not exactly groom me for Harvard. My
mother used to call the television set the "idiot box" — an apt
description. But as innocuous as those shows were, they would
never contradict basic family values. Sexual activity was private
and sacred. People in love got married. Children were considered a blessing, not a curse. Words were careful and not vulgar.

Lying, cheating, and disrespect were considered wrong. They supported the culture of Camelot.

Please don't misunderstand my reflections as mere nostalgia. Camelot was far from perfect. Neighborhoods were homogenous and racially restrictive. Church policy and a priest's personal opinion had the same weight as dogma. Social mores were often synonymous with morals and were as inflexible as granite. Still, it provided an environment that was supportive of family and conducive to traditional faith.

I remember reading a poster entitled "All I Really Need to Know I Learned in Kindergarten." Its words were taken from a book by Robert Fulghum. He wrote that the most important things were not learned in college, but in the simple lessons taught in childhood, such as "taking naps every afternoon," and "sticking together." But my kindergarten of Camelot gave even more essential truths, including:

Jesus loves you.
You are made in the image and likeness of God.
You will die someday, but you can live forever in Heaven.
Pray everyday.

These truths kept me on the *crossways* to Christ. Be it summer showers or fall floods, there was no storm Jesus couldn't calm. Jesus was *the* Man for all seasons.

But as I grew older, the cracks in my voice were matched by cracks in the Catholic castle walls. Unable to withstand assaults from the outside, rival ways to truth and happiness began to appear. As my adulthood self began to wax, my childhood faith began to wane. Like many others of my generation, innocence gave way to pretense, form began to be valued over substance, and lifestyle became the priority instead of life.

Thanks to the Second Vatican Council, Catholics began the much-needed process of learning about other religions and seeing the good that was beyond our Catholic community. But in the process, some Catholics stopped searching for the truth within their own faith. They sought the value of other ways without first understanding their own. Armed with only a *child's* understanding of faith, they encountered sophisticated *adult* world-views. John XXIII challenged us to open the windows of the Church to let the spiritual "fresh air" in, to seek a common ground and a common humanity. But some Catholics forgot to put a screen on the open window. Consequently, the once-insulated family got bombarded with the "dirt" of hedonism, materialism, etc. "Doing your own thing" replaced doing "God's thing," with many Catholics lacking the words or wisdom to intellectually do battle with falsehoods advertised in attractive modern designs.

This change is echoed in the media culture of today. We have gone from a stern moral code to Howard Stern. We've replaced the Madonna with "Madonna." Rock lyrics celebrate violence and sadomasochism. Serial killers are marketed like baseball cards. Pornography is but "three clicks" of a computer mouse away. This era has been called "the information age," but it more accurately could be called "the misinformation age," for whoever controls the means used to impart information and entertainment has power. And this power has been less than benign. It is a power that has ripped through the walls of the Catholic castle and distorted our ideas of Christ and ourselves. It has even attacked our most sacred treasure — the child. Children today have *access to excess* in a way I never could have dreamed of in the 1960's and 70's. Might, political or electronic, has begun to make right. The media Mordred has come to Camelot.

But despite any of these ominous cultural changes, grace continues to work through it all. Countless men still honor their wives. Mothers still hold their precious babies tight. Candles are lit and Santa Claus continues his rounds. Many a knee still bends in prayer to the Almighty. Children still delight and inspire.

Despite the cacophony of noise around me, through the love of many friends and family members, I even managed to strain my ears and hear the celestial music of Jesus, and reconnect with the symphony begun in my childhood. I became a knight of the Christian roundtable. My second childhood had begun.

If your heart has led your mind back to the *crossways*, then let the following reflections be my gift to you. If these words do not fire up your mind or warm your heart, then feel free to either burn them or return them for a toaster oven. This book is designed to help "re-mind" my generation of essential Catholic Christian principles. I believe that each of us needs to courageously seek the light of Christ. As Plato said:

> *We can easily forgive a child who is afraid of the dark;*
> *The real tragedy of life is when adults are afraid of the*
> *light.*

As we walk the crossways to Christ, each of us should not only strive to become the "body of Christ," but also the "mind of Christ" as well. I hope these words can weave an adult understanding into the fabric of childlike faith. I seek here not to *inform* the mind but help *form* it. It is written for the young — the young at heart.

Each section of this book contains twelve reflections. The first part, *The Way of **Faith***, reflects on the mystery of divinity and our relationship with God. The second segment, *The Way of **Love***, reflects on the mystery of humanity and our relationships with others. Just as the horizontal and vertical beams of the cross meet in the center, as the colors blue and red blend into purple, so too the way of faith and love merge in Christ. The final section, *The Way of **Discipleship***, reflects on the mystery of Christ and our relationship with Him. Each of these reflections is like the stone David prepared for battle with Goliath — aimed at the head, but meant for the heart.

Part One:

THE VERTICAL CROSSBEAM
The Mystery of Divinity and Our Relationship to God

THE WAY OF FAITH

Title	Theme
1. Candlelight	Life and Death
2. Rain	Suffering
3. Nighttime	Meaning of Life
4. Copernicus	Existence of God
5. The Rose	God and Meaning
6. Brothers	Faith and Science
7. Comets	Miracles
8. Tractor Beams	Nature of Religion
9. Moonlight	Idolatry
10. Starship Enterprise	Nature of the World
11. The Mountain	Nature of Prayer
12. The Field	Heaven

Candlelight

"Therefore I tell you, do not worry about your life, what you will eat or drink, or about your body, what you will wear. Is not life more than food and the body more than clothing? … Do not worry about tomorrow; tomorrow will take care of itself."   Matthew 6:25, 34a

The room is floating in family and friends. The walls are painted in multicolored balloons. The lights are dimmed. All that can be seen is shadows, smiles and candle glow. A cake centers the table. A song of birthday praise, a wish to make, and with a gust of breath, candles are blown out. The candlelight is gone… but there is light that remains.

Life is a movement from one light to another. From our conception in the womb until the time of our birth, all we know is darkness. With our birth, we are introduced to incredible light. From birthday to birthday, as we move through the years, we live in another kind of darkness. In our death — our rebirth, we are introduced to the incredible Light.

Imagine for a moment the thoughts and experiences of a male fetus inside his mother's womb. He lives in pervasive darkness, and he is comfortable with it. He cannot see his mother face to face, even though her presence surrounds him. She is holding him so close that he cannot get a complete picture of what his mother looks like. Mom isn't one object in the amniotic sac; she is the maker of his world. She is in everything he sees and is much more that he doesn't see. He receives food everyday, though he can't explain fully the miracle of how it comes

3

to him. The womb provides many blessings, and it works according to a brilliant design, which points to the existence of a mother. He has seen brief instances of light, though in his darkness he has never seen the outside world. When his birth-day finally arrives, he leaves the only safe comfortable world that he has ever known. From his point of view, it would seem like dying, and he is dying to that world. But if he has faith, he will trust that his mother will take care of him. And a *child is born* into the light of the world. On that day, he shall finally see his mother face to face.

We live in the pervasive darkness of sin, evil, disease, and death, yet some of us are comfortable in the darkness. We cannot see God our Father face to face, though His presence surrounds us. God holds us so close to Himself that we cannot get a complete picture of what He looks like. God is not one object in the universe; He is the creator of the world. God is in everything we see and is much more that we do not see. We receive food everyday, though we can't explain fully the miracle of how food comes to be. Nature provides many blessings; and the universe works according to a brilliant design, which points to the existence of a Father. We have seen brief miraculous instances of eternal light, though in our darkness we have never seen the next world. When our day of death finally arrives, we leave the only safe comfortable world that we have ever known. From our point of view, it seems like dying, and we are dying to this world. But if we have faith, we will trust that our Father will take care of us. And a *child is born-again* into the Light of the World. On that day, we shall finally see our Father, face to face.

Birthday parties are humbling, for often it is harder to accept praise than it is to give it. This is especially true with birthdays, because we are celebrating something completely out of our control. We didn't choose the moment of our birth, let alone the day, nor the family we were born into. We didn't select our parents, we didn't pick our fingerprints, and we didn't survey our era of history before we entered it. We are characters in a great story, but we're not the Author. Chapter One, our birth, was written by God and others. Slowly but surely, as we pass by birthday after birthday, God allows us to interact with the author Himself, and have a voice in our own story. With our first birthday, we had no control. But with our final birthday, the day of our passage through death, what occurs is largely up to us. For sometime between birthday celebrations, God will ask us to accept that God is God and we are not. And the choice we make shapes our destiny. This is the essence of the word *religion* — it comes from the Latin *"religare"* — to bind together. We can choose to bind ourselves together with God. To be religious is to see ourselves as creation and not the Creator.

Our task on earth is to keep the candlelight of faith, hope, and love burning within our lives, as we move from birth-light to eternal-light. As our bodies grow older, moving further away from our first birthday, our souls can grow younger, moving closer towards our second birthday.

Yet it is amazing that what children long for, their birthdays, some adults dread. They dread their birthdays because it reminds them of their age, and age reminds them of the inevitability of death. So they cling to the American "youth culture" that markets the illusion of immortality and promotes the denial of death. They hide the elderly in unseen rooms, dye away the gray hair, and surgically remove the wrinkles. But birthdays, the natural signposts along the journey of life, remind them of their foolishness and rekindle their fear. They look back to the past and see the candlelight flickering, appearing dimmer with each passing year. If only they could see the light that lies ahead.

Faith is the only real antidote to fear. For faith reveals that life is not a journey from womb to tomb, but rather a voyage from womb to heavenly womb. Once life is seen as the movement from light to Eternal light, then we can become like Merlin. For those not familiar with the Arthurian legend, Merlin was a wizard and instructor to the once and future King Arthur. Merlin had great wisdom because he lived *backwards*. As others aged, he *youthened*. As fantastic as this may seem, it is not that far from our grasp. If we can tap ourselves into the divine, creative, and playful vitality of God, our souls can stay young with wonder and enthusiasm, even while our bodies age. Like Merlin, we can *youthen* as we move toward "the one who makes all things new." Birthdays, therefore, are not trap doors, they are steps leading closer and closer towards an incredible light. It will be a light unlike any we have ever experienced. It might even be painful at first, as we adjust to its penetrating power. But soon, we can drink it in to us as though it were liquid light — a fountain of eternal youth — resurrecting not only our soul but our body as well. No doubt God our Father will offer it to us in the humble cup of a carpenter from Galilee.

So light the candles on the cake. Their glow serves to remind us of the promise of a future light that can cast no shadows. Jesus' call to us in life is: *Come along with Me, for the best is yet to be.* The time we are here in the shadowlands can be a time of hope and celebration, if we can hold on to this central religious principle: Life is God's birthday gift to us, and what we do with it, is our gift to God. And grave concerns become youthful delight.

❧

A birthday does not come merely to remind a man
that he has been born. It comes that he may be born again.
G.K. CHESTERTON

6

Rain

"I know that you can do all things, and that no purpose of yours can be hindered. I have dealt with great things that I do not understand; things too wonderful for me, which I cannot know." Job 42:2-3

Rain falls — a cold, wet rain that soaks us and chills us to the bone. Blue-black storm clouds darken our life. Suffering and horror rain upon the just and the unjust, the innocent drown and the guilty find refuge, murder and cancer strike like lightning, suicide and tragedy flood our world, and we ask the question, "Why?"

Maybe a rainfall of suffering indicates that there is no God. Because God would have to be perfect, a perfect God would create a perfect world. But the world is definitely not perfect. So God is either not all-powerful, since He couldn't create a perfect world, or not all-loving, since He could have created a perfect world but He didn't. Either way, He is not perfect. Therefore, there is no God.

Not a bad argument. We had better be able to answer this one. If we cannot find a meaning in suffering, we will not find meaning at all. The premise is correct. A perfect God *would* create a perfect world. The flaw in this atheist argument lies in the inference that God did not create a perfect world. God did create a perfect world! He created one that was so perfect, that He gave the world the power to choose whether or not it wanted to remain perfect. God gave this world a piece of Himself — His freedom — so that we could choose freely our own destiny.

7

We could choose to love God in return, and stay in peace and joy, or we could choose to be gods ourselves, and bring sin, evil, and suffering into the world. God wanted His creature "man" to have the capacity for love. And love must be freely chosen or it is not love. As we have discovered, we can't make someone love us; they have to choose love for themselves. Could God destroy all the sin and evil in the world? — In a heartbeat. God could destroy Satan with the batting of one of His eyelashes. It wouldn't even be a contest. But He won't, for now. If God destroys evil, He destroys free will. If God destroys free will, He destroys the possibility of love — the only thing that makes life meaningful — and He won't do that! God loves us too much to destroy free will. Therefore, He allows unearned suffering and pain in our lives. Freedom... what a wonderful gift. Yet it is freedom that contains the source of suffering... and the world is *Paradise Lost*.

The mystery of free will and love provide the beginning of a rational answer to the rational question "Why?" But rarely is the question asked in a spirit of rationality. Suffering is not a problem of the intellect but of the will. When suffering rains down upon us, anger, frustration, and bewilderment fill us. We ask "Why?" from the depths of our being. We want healing, not a supernatural explanation. We want escape, not acceptance. We want peace, not logic. We want relief, not theology. We want shelter from the rain, not a weather forecast.

If theology can offer any help at all, it lies in our being able to understand suffering. Suffering is not a problem, it is a mystery. Human reason alone cannot provide the answer. We cannot find the answer on a printed page. Words will not suffice, but *the Word* will. Faith can take us through the natural clouds of darkness to see the supernatural brightness on their other side. I cannot write the answer to the mystery of suffering, but we each can meet *the Answer*.

We are caught in storms not of our own making, calling out to a God who will not remove them. If we turn to secular culture, they will tell us to escape the rain and escape the pain. Suffering is evil and meaningless. Life is all clouds and darkness with occasions of light coming from us. They will offer technological "umbrellas" to separate ourselves from legitimate suffering — assisted suicide, legal abortion, recreational drugs, nihilistic entertainment, euthanasia — all of which only compound human misery and confound the human soul.

But having said that God allows suffering is not to say that He is aloof and removed from the solution. Technological transformation is not the answer, but spiritual transformation is. He will not remove it, but He has made all suffering potentially good. Suffering can bring humility. Suffering can teach. Through suffering we can grow. Suffering is the human-imposed bitter medicine we need to become healed of our sinful disease. Life is not all darkness. It only appears dark to us because we are blinded by God's infinite radiance. One day the veil of tears will be lifted. One day the rain will end and the reign will begin.

Let it rain. Throw down our umbrellas of fear. Stand out in it and let it fall upon us. Drink it in. Laugh, scream, cry, shout out in anger at God — but hold on. Let it hit us, let it hurt us, soak us, even drown us. We will not be out there alone. The Man who slept through storms on the Sea of Galilee is with us. We need not be afraid. He will stand with us, arm in arm. He will carry us when we can stand no longer. God has Himself entered the rainstorm. We need only to look deep down inside ourselves, and face the rain. Choose hope in the midst of despair. Stop asking "Why?" and start asking "How?" Find a reason, a purpose, a meaning in the suffering and we can transcend it. Unearned suffering can be redemptive. Turn the suffering rain into the waters of a baptism. Let it kill us, and we will be reborn. Suffering cannot hurt us — our bodies maybe, but not us. Pain cannot damage the soul unless we allow it. We are free. The very freedom that is the source of suffering, that keeps the rain falling, can also provide a solution to suffering — and the world becomes

Paradise Found. It is the fierce storms that make the river flow. It is the hard rains that water the fields. It is the rain of suffering that can thaw our icy hearts and melt away arrogance and ignorance. Rainfall can leave the air fresh and clear, to let the world begin again.

A perfect world… no. But a world transformed to provide the chance for humanity to become perfect. We are not here to feel good, we are here to become good. Suffering is endemic to the human condition. Why doesn't God do something about evil? He has — He has made us. Let the struggle begin. Why doesn't God do something about suffering? He has — He has transformed it and conquered it. He has not eliminated it. We cannot solve the mystery of suffering but it can solve us. Let the rain fall. Words cannot end suffering or bring the dead back to life, but *the Word made flesh* can. He is *Son*shine through the pouring rain.

❧

Pain drips upon the heart, as against our will.
And even in our own despite, comes wisdom
From the awful grace of the gods.

AESCHYLUS

Nighttime

"My God, my God, why have you abandoned me? Why so far from my cries for help, from my cries of anguish?"
Psalm 22:2a

Sometimes when we are alone, and the dark of night surrounds us, the darkness of doubt finds a way inside. And we feel the distance between God and ourselves. Even religious people don't always feel religious. We pray to God and long for just a whisper from Him, but He doesn't audibly answer us. We long to see God, but we can't see through this cloud of unknowing. If He is out there, He seems far away. God is invisible, inaudible, and intangible. No wonder we drift away. We sense a gulf of uncertainty, a chasm of confusion, an abyss of darkness between God and us. Spiritual persons refer to this as "the dark night of the soul." We feel abandoned. Questions begin to rise up from inside us.

Does God exist? Is God a person? If God exists, where is He? God sometimes seems only as real as a fairy tale. We call out but He doesn't answer. We wait but He never shows. If only we could be certain. Why doesn't He just show Himself? If God really wants us to know about Him, why doesn't He just plainly, clearly, demonstrably, reveal Himself to us? Then we could see Him with our eyes, hear His voice, and touch His hand. Everyone could then follow Him without doubt and uncertainty. *Then we would be satisfied. Then we would believe in God!*

But would God be satisfied? Would God believe in us? Maybe

"Does God exist?" is the wrong question. Maybe we are not in this world to ask God this question, maybe we are here to answer God's question, *"Does Man exist?"* We want God to meet our demands and show Himself plainly. But a real God would not be subject to our demands. He would do the demanding, not us. If God fit Himself into our little formula for belief, then God is not really in charge. The children would be controlling the Parent. Perhaps God our Father is trying to teach His children something. Perhaps He wants us to grow! We have all seen a mother hold her eight month-old child by the hands, teaching her the sensation of walking. She is encouraging her first step, never satisfied with just crawling. God is like a human parent with us, pleased but never satisfied, teaching us to walk instead of to crawl. With this in mind, let's consider a different answer to the question, "Why doesn't God just show Himself visibly to everyone so that there would be no doubt?"

God could. But He doesn't. If He appeared before everyone, to be verified with eyes and ears, to be touched with hands, we would know God the same way animals know anything — through their senses. But what if God didn't intend us to be merely like the other animals? What if He made us to be *more* than an animal? Maybe God wants us to rely on "another" part of ourselves to come to know Him, a part that we find harder to trust, just as a young baby does not trust her feet at first when learning to walk. God doesn't want to test our eyes — they are just a physical trait, a gift from God but temporary and limited. God wants to test our "eyes" of faith — that is a spiritual trait, a gift from God but enduring and unlimited. God is trying to help us become the kind of creature that is like Himself, one that can know boundless joy and eternal life. So He wants us to become more divine and spiritual, while we want to remain more animal and physical. So the *real* question becomes, once again, *"Does Man exist?"* Are we willing to become the kind of human that God wants us to be?

12

God is our Father, He is the parent we need, and not the parent we want. God is also quite clever. He created a world that, if we look at it *only* through our natural senses, we can see no visibly clear sign of His existence. This is why atheists and agnostics see religion as such a fantasy. "Prove it to me!" they demand, seeking sensory verification from a God who will not provide it.

At the same time, if we choose to use our more intangible gifts of faith and love, in other words, if we "look" at the world through our supernatural senses, we can see overwhelming, obvious, incredible signs of God all around us! The world seems to be "shouting" out God's existence. Our mind applies reason to this gift of faith, and God's existence becomes the most logical conclusion that can be drawn. Our experience, looking through the created world to the meaning behind, sees God everywhere. Every brook is babbling His name. Every lark is whistling His voice. Every tree is the hand of the earth, reaching upwards to the heavens. Every person we love is showing us His heart.

Blaise Pascal, a French Christian of the 17th century observed this contrast of worldviews.

> ... he (God) has qualified our knowledge of him by giving signs which can be seen only by those who seek and not by those who do not. There is enough light for those who desire only to see, and enough darkness for those of a contrary disposition.

God has given us a world that allows for a real choice. Choose faith, and the world becomes illuminated with His presence. Choose doubt, and the world remains in dark ignorance to His presence.

The answer to our ultimate question of the dark night of the soul, *"Does God exist?"* is first another question. What kind of person do we choose to become? Will we revert back to our

13

senses alone, even though they can deceive us and will eventually cease to function? Or will we rely on faith, hope, and love, which can sustain us and never fail us? To put it simply, we must answer for ourselves the question; *"Does Man exist?"* Or would we rather be a mouse? In a wonderful book called *The Little Prince*, Antoine de Saint-Exupery asks us this same question. Set as an adult fable, Saint-Exupery tells the story of a little prince who travels from solitary planet to solitary planet, seeking an answer that will give his life meaning. On Earth, he finds in his friendship with a fox that the twofold gift of faith and love *is* the answer. So the little prince offers up his life to return to his home planet, to care for his beloved flower that he had abandoned many years before, and to faithfully protect his rose from a sheep that might try to eat her. The narrator of the story, a pilot who had befriended the little prince, remains on earth, struggling to choose whether or not his life will be one of faith and love. Sometimes he believes that the little prince is back on his planet caring for his flower, and his faith and love gives him great comfort and meaning. At other times he despairs, thinking that the sheep might have eaten the flower, doubting the little prince's faithfulness, and this gives him great sorrow and meaninglessness. Then the pilot turns and addresses us in the final words of the fable, and offers us the same choice.

> *Look up at the sky. Ask yourselves: Is it yes or no?*
> *Has the sheep eaten the flower?*
> *And you will see how everything changes...*
> *And no grown-up will ever understand that this is a matter*
> *of utmost importance!*

Will we choose to be a "man" and develop the gifts that we have been given, those of faith and love, and find meaning and joy in life? Or will we choose to be less than a "man" and doubt the gifts we have been given, and know meaninglessness and sorrow in life? Each of us must choose, and that choice will become our destiny.

In the dark night of the soul, we must choose to become the bright knight of the soul, and have the courage to become more than what we are now. We do not have to go it alone. There is *the* Bright Knight; He is the Dayspring that pierced through the abyss of darkness. He showed us how to reach dawn. He taught us that night is not the end. The chasm of confusion can be bridged. The gulf of uncertainty can be crossed. The cloud of unknowing can be cleared by the Morning Son. The night is offering us a chance to deepen and renew our faith and strengthen our reliance on love. As a knight of faith, we will make it through the dark night of the soul and on to daybreak.

❧

If the thought comes to you that anything you have
thought about God is mistaken and that there is
no God, do not be dismayed. It happens to
many people. This (thought) comes from
the fact that there was something wrong with your
belief, and you must strive to grasp better
that which you call God.

LEO TOLSTOY

Copernicus

One star differs from another star in glory.

1 Corinthians 15:41

Long, long ago, there lived an astronomer named Mikolaj. He had dedicated his life's work to search for the answer to a question: *What is the center of the known physical universe? What lies at the core of everything we see?* Mikolaj believed that if he could just resolve this question, many more answers about humanity and the world, would be found. So Mikolaj looked to the stars and reflected on the world around him. He looked backward to move forward. He relied on the authority of those who had gone before him, most particularly a scientist named Ptolemy of Alexandria of the second century, and then drew his own conclusions.

Mikolaj, who eventually became known as Copernicus, attacked the prevailing notion of the day, which held that the earth was the center of the universe and the sun and planets revolved around it. This was called the geocentric, earth-centered view of the universe. Everyone who was anyone in 16th century Europe believed this — it was intellectually fashionable. But Copernicus sought the truth. He believed that the sun was at the center and the earth and other planets revolved around it. He was not trying to devalue the earth, he simply believed that we would never know the earth's true nature unless it was put into proper perspective. But before he could prove it, he had to prove himself worthy of higher learning. So he studied diplomacy, mathematics, linguistics, art, medicine, and canon law, in addition to learning the scientific work of his predecessors. This he combined with his own observations of the world around him. The Copernican theory, which he called the heliocentric, sun-centered view of the universe, was finally published in 1543 under the title *De revolutionibus*. It eventually became the foundation for all modern astronomy. Copernicus had begun a scientific revolution in how we think about ourselves and the universe we live in.

Mikolaj's search is not unlike our search for answers. We too, must dedicate our life to search for the answer to a spiritual question. *What is the center of the universe? What lies at the core of everything we see?* If we could just resolve this question, many more answers about ourselves and the world would be found. And so we must look to the stars and reflect on the world around us. And we, too, must look backward to move forward. We can rely on the authority of those who have gone before us, most particularly a teacher named Jesus of Nazareth of the first century, and then draw our own conclusions.

Does God exist? Is He at the center of our universe? Just as Copernicus had made his own observations and had learned the wisdom of those who had gone before him, we can as well. We must fearlessly ask the great questions and prove ourselves worthy of higher learning, and study the way of wisdom that has gone before us. Having accepted the gift of faith, we see that faith uses reason to seek understanding. Clues have been left for the clueless, and the seasons have given reasons for the God we seek.

Design. When we look at a painting, we would not normally conclude that the picture formed as a result of a random spilling of paint. The ordered design presupposes a designer. Looking at nature, it becomes clear that there is an intelligent design to the universe. Where there is a design, there must be a designer. The universe's intricate design points to a *Universal Designer…* God. God would not be limited by what He designed. As St.

Irenaeus said, "For nature reveals its Author, the work suggests the Artist, and the world manifests its Designer."

Causality. As we observe the way objects relate to one another, we see that nothing ever causes itself. For every effect we see, there is always a cause behind it. Matter is pretty "wimpy," for it is always dependent on something else to cause it. Upon reaching age two, all my daughters discovered cause and effect: "Why do we eat? Why is their air? Why is the grass green?" They almost "caused" insanity in their poor father! Since the natural universe exists and is totally dependent, there must be an independent *super*natural cause for the universe that exists outside the universe, a *First Cause,* an *Uncaused Cause*... God. The universe itself couldn't be the First Cause because nothing in it causes itself. Since God is supernatural, He would not be subject to the natural cause and effect rule. He started and invented this process. The Ruler is not subject to His own rules.

Morality. Looking at human nature, we see that everyone in the world experiences an obligation to be good. We don't always obey because we are free to refuse to do so, and we don't always completely agree on the rules, but we all experience an obligation, regardless of history or culture. This moral law is not merely a social contract among people, for sometimes we use it to judge our man-made laws to be unjust. This moral law comes from a source that is higher than human laws. The only possible and reasonable source for moral law is a *Moral Lawgiver*... God. The great writer Fyodor Dostoevsky realized this necessary connection between religion and morality when he wrote: "If there is no God, then everything is permissible."

Meaning. Humanity has always believed that life has an ultimate purpose and meaning. It would not be logical for us to create meaning for ourselves if there truly is no ultimate meaning to life. Death makes "human-invented meaning" meaningless. But inside each of us, there lies the conviction that life is indeed meaningful. But if life is a story, then there must be a

Storyteller... God. As G.K. Chesterton succinctly stated, "I had always felt life first as a story: and if there is a story, there is a storyteller."

It is our task to attack the prevailing notion of the day — that each of us is the center of the universe and everyone else should revolve around us. This can be called the egocentric, self-centered view of the universe. Everyone who is anyone in 21st century America has been exposed to this — it is fashionable. But like Copernicus, Christians must seek the truth. In faith, we believe that God exists. And reason and human experience supports this claim. God is at the center of the universe. He lies at the core of everything seen and unseen. We are not trying to devalue human beings, we simply believe that we will never know our true nature until we understand our rightful place and see our position in proper perspective.

But unlike Copernicus, who began a scientific revolution, we have an advantage. We can follow the Man who *was* a spiritual Revolution. Our religious Copernicus has come. And He has proposed a theocentric, Christ-centered view of the universe. The answer lies not in a problem but in a Person. Jesus is *the* Answer. And we will only come to know ourselves when we make him the center of our lives. For Christians revolve around the *Son*.

❧

Faith is a habit of mind, which begins eternal life in us, and induces a reasonable assent to things unseen.
THOMAS AQUINAS

The Rose

For if we believe that Jesus died and rose, so too will God, through Jesus, bring with him those who have fallen asleep. 1 Thessalonians 4:14

In the film *Dead Poets Society*, students at a prestigious prep school begin their year by meeting their new literature teacher, Mr. Keating (played by Robin Williams). He leads his class out into the hallway and has them look closely at class portraits of former students from yesteryear. "Look at them, gentlemen," Keating instructs, "These men are pushing up daffodils. They are food for worms. But they have an important message to give you. Listen closely." Keating then whispers in his students' ears as they gaze upon the faces of once-youthful men, "*C-a-r-p-e... c-a-r-p-e d-i-e-m*... seize the day... make your lives extraordinary!"

To summarize Keating's lesson: "Life ends in death. While we're alive, 'gather up rosebuds while ye may,' because there is no second chance. The roses die and so do we. Seek happiness everyday and suck the marrow out of life. Live now while we still can, not for the future. "Dead"icated poets lived extraordinary lives, so should we." This philosophy was not invented for the film. The *carpe diem* philosophy was championed by men like Oscar Wilde around the turn of the last century. It is an appealing sentiment, a motivational discourse. It is also incomplete, and therefore a reckless and dangerous theology! What appears harmless on the surface can be deadly underneath.

Were I a student in Keating's class, I might have raised my

hand and asked two questions. "Mr. Keating, *how* and *why?*" First, *how* are we to seize the day? *Carpe diem* gives no guidelines. Should we live for truth and goodness, or lies and pleasure? Can we seize the day for ourselves without regard to others? If the day is mine, then I own it and I decide what is right and wrong, and life is my personal quest for happiness. If we gather rose-buds, will we not find thorns? And won't gathering rosebuds for ourselves only hasten their death? As an old song said:

> *Love is a rose but you better not pick it,*
> *it only grows when it's on the vine.*
> *A handful of thorns and you know you've missed it.*
> *You lose your love when you say the word "mine."*

And even more importantly, *why* should we seize the day? If everything that we ever do only ends in meaningless death, then everything we do is meaningless. To put it mathematically, if daily positive moments X+Y+Z all add up to *zero*, then X, Y, and Z are zeroes as well! If nothing lasts, then nothing matters. Why should I have children? So they can grow up to discover the horror of meaningless death for themselves? What's the point in living at all? "To be or not to be, that is the question." Keating tells us "to be" despite the fact that we are inevitably "not to be." If the grave is our ultimate end, corpses rotting in the ground, then we are like Sisyphus in hell. From Greek mythology, a king named Sisyphus was condemned to roll a heavy boulder up a large hill, only to see it roll back down the other side... and then roll it up again and again... forever! Would we tell Sisyphus to "seize the day," and make the most of his rock and roll world? I hardly think so, but the *carpe diem* philosophy tells us to do the same. *If* death is the final curtain, then Macbeth was right, and "life is a tale told by an idiot, full of sound and fury, signifying... nothing!" The universe has evolved for billions of years to produce Man, a sentient being who is self-aware, and we just die and decay until the planet blows up! Then life is a cosmic abortion and philosophers like Nietzsche were correct: life is thorns without petals, meaningless and worthless. Nietzsche died a lunatic, a fitting response to an absurd and empty world.

But death isn't the end. Deep in our hearts, we will not accept that life is meaningless. There is a drive for meaning within us. Every fiber of our being rails against this shroud of death. We cannot accept this fate and then just "seize the day" with no rhyme or reason. And therein lies our hope and faith in God and the resurrection of Jesus. If God exists, then it is possible that He, who lives forever, can aid us who long to live forever. The question "to be or not to be," can be better phrased as "God or not God, that is the question." If there truly *is* a God, then there is an ultimate plan and purpose — life has infinite meaning! If there is not a God, then life is meaningless, and it would be absurd to strive for meaning anyway. If "God or not God" is the question, then what's the answer?

Jesus is the perfect answer. If Jesus of Nazareth really did rise from the dead, then He is the Son of God! Love crucified, arose! God has defeated death and He beckons us to follow, with the chance to live forever with Him. Then the resurrection moment in history is our hope fulfilled, our faith vindicated. Life, proclaimed the early Christians, is infinitely meaningful. What we do with our lives matters not merely to us. It matters to God. The ultimate God has given us ultimate purpose and meaning. Love is stronger than death. Hope springs eternal. Faith lives forever. So can we. Our grave concerns can be buried, we can spring to new life like a winter rose, shrouded only in love in the Kingdom of God.

Christianity did away with the *carpe diem* philosophy about two thousand years ago. The great British Catholic writer and apologist, G.K. Chesterton, understood this:

> But the carpe diem *religion is not the religion of happy people, but of very unhappy people. Great joy does not*

The Rose

gather the rosebuds while it may; its eyes are fixed on
the immortal rose (Mary and/or Christ) that Dante saw.

Chesterton knew that the "day" is not ours to seize. This day the Lord has made. We can live *in* the moment, rather than *for* the moment. Through Him we live each moment to the fullest, not to achieve happiness, but to act with goodness and do what brings meaning. We cannot pursue happiness. The more we do, the more it eludes us. It comes to us when we are engaged in meaningful endeavors. When I think about the times in my life when I was most happy, they were times when I was *least* conscious of trying to be happy! We do not enjoy the moment for the sake of the moment itself; we enjoy it when we value someone or something within the moment. Personal happiness cannot be our goal; it will only evade us if we make it our priority. Knowing, loving, and serving God must be our goal. Happiness will find us, we need not search for it. Language scholars must forgive my attempt at a word play in Latin, but we should not *carpe diem*, but rather *carpe Deum*... we should seize God! Or more precisely, we should allow God to seize us. Only then can we see the infinite value of all that we are and do, and the ultimate meaningfulness of life.

Nor will focusing only on the present moment give us the happiness we seek. According to Victor Frankl, a psychiatrist who wrote of his experiences in a Nazi concentration camp in the book *Man's Search for Meaning*: "It is the peculiarity of man that he can only live by looking into the future... the prisoner who had lost faith in the future — his future — was doomed." Contrary to the *carpe diem* philosophy, Frankl understood the importance of a future goal to give meaning to the present. Prisoners who "lived only for the day" did not survive. Nor will we. Our future goal of heaven, properly understood, does not rob us of the treasures within the present. In fact, the goal of reaching eternal heaven can give infinite meaning to the present.

The challenge for Christians is to learn from the past, live in the present, and envision the future. The *rose* can remind us of past events, and of a future promise yet to come. There is a legend, mentioned by St. Ambrose, that the rose first grew in Paradise, without thorns. After the fall, the rose took thorns as a reminder of sin and our fall from grace, while its fragrance and beauty continued to remind us of a future Paradise. As Christians, we do not "gather up roses while we may." Roses off the vine wither and die, as do we. So we place our faith in *the Immortal Rose* who rose from the dead and can lead us to Paradise. He will gather us. He took on our thorns and made them a crown. His infinite roots lie buried in a world we cannot yet see. *The Immortal Rose*, by any other name, is Jesus Christ. We must *carpe Deum*, seize God — making each day extraordinary in love. The meaning of life will bloom within us when we look at life through "immortal rose-colored glasses."

❧

In a last violent protest against the hopelessness of imminent death, I sensed my spirit piercing through the enveloping gloom. I felt it transcend that hopeless, meaningless world, and from somewhere I heard a victorious "Yes" in answer to my question of the existence of an ultimate purpose.

VICTOR FRANKL

Brothers

Faith is the substance of things hoped for and evidence of things unseen.   Hebrews 11:1

A man had fallen off the edge of a high cliff. He managed to grab onto the root of a tree growing out of the side of the cliff and was hanging on for dear life. He began to pray. Then he heard the voice of God asking him:
"Do you really believe in me?"
"I do!" *protested the poor man whose life hung in the balance.*
"Do you trust me?" *asked the voice of God.*
"Yes! Yes!" *the man answered.*
Then the voice of God came back: "Then I will see to it that you are saved. Now, do what I tell you to do. Now... let go!"

From *A Reason to Live, A Reason to Die*, John Powell, SJ

Faith is a matter of trust. Particularly, *faith* is belief and trust in God, and commitment to Him even though God is too infinite for us to be able to fully understand Him. Without having all the answers, without absolute certainty, we must leap, we must let go. God has carried us in past. He will uphold us always. He will not let go.

This is the ultimate risk with an ultimate payoff. But faith is not the sole possession of religious individuals alone. Everyone has some degree of faith, though not everyone is willing to allow faith to help them say "yes" to the question of God, they

25

use faith nonetheless to sow meaningful threads that hold together the complicated pattern of life. Consider the following statements. *None* of them can be scientifically proven. They *all* require some level of faith:

- At this moment, my senses are accurately presenting me reality.
- Science is the only way to know anything for certain.
- The scientific method is the way to determine fact.
- I am thinking of the color blue.

- My parents love me.
- We should strive to speak and act truthfully in friendship.
- My wife will be faithful to me in marriage, until death we do part.

- Women are equal to men in basic human rights and dignity.
- Black men and women are persons, therefore slavery is wrong.
- Unborn children are persons whose lives should be legally protected.

- God exists, (not just in my mind but in reality).
- God is a divine Person, not a force.
- Jesus Christ rose from the dead.
- The Catholic Church is guided by the Holy Spirit.

- There is no God; I am master of my own fate.
- I am not certain there is a God.

Some of these statements are easily agreed upon, others are far more controversial, but they *all* require faith! The first set of four is philosophical, and can be assumed by people without much reflection. Yet we see in these statements that even *science* is predicated on some reasonable assertions of *faith*. For example, we cannot use the scientific method to prove the scientific method; that would be illogical. We have to believe in the method before we can accept the conclusions derived from it. Some leap of faith, either in our senses or in a tool of science, is necessary to begin science at all. The second set involves interpersonal relationships and intangible attributes to which many of us aspire, such as truth and love. We cannot prove the existence of truth and love, but they are real. Most children take a leap of faith and believe that their parents love them. Some are not able. Many adults take the walk of faith down the wedding aisle of marriage. Some do not. It's a matter of commitment; choosing to place trust in yourself and in another person. The third set are moral issues, some commonly agreed upon, some still hotly debated. But they all require a faith capacity to believe in *justice*, a nonscientific quality not found in a test tube. We can see justice working through a situation, but we cannot see justice itself.

The remaining statements deal with religious issues. The first statement requires a choice of the will to "go the distance" in faith to believe and trust in God. The next three statements involve faith in a particular understanding of God's nature and revelation. The last two statements of unbelief, surprisingly, involve some level of faith as well. The agnostic professes a *faith* in his doubts rather than in God. The atheist *believes* in his unbelief, and unwittingly, ends up *having faith* in a god — namely himself.

So we see that faith is endemic to the human condition. It is inescapable. René Descartes, a philosopher of the 17th century, summarized his view of the reality of his being with the phrase, *cogito ergo sum — I think, therefore I am.* But even before thinking takes place, our eyes and other senses provide our minds with information from the real world. When we accept that sensory information as being accurate, we are making an immediate intuitive leap of faith. So even our thinking involves implicit faith! Perhaps Descartes' phrase should be replaced with a better one: *credo ergo sum* — *I believe, therefore I am.* Our capacity for faith and how we use this capacity defines who we are. There is an often-used saying that illustrates the importance of faith:

Faith gives us real eyes *to* realize *where the* real lies.

Applying reason and personal experience to the supernatural world of *faith* gives us theology, morality, etc. Applying reason and empirical observation to the natural world of *science* gives us biology, astronomy, etc. Faith is the big brother of science, for even science requires some intuitive leaps of faith in order to study the physical world. But in the minds of some in the modern world, there is a division, a quarrel, between faith and science — an intellectual "Cain and Abel" conflict that has caused these two brothers to oppose one another, rather than work together towards a common goal.

Throughout history, religious authority has occasionally tried to influence the results of scientific analysis. This *religious elitism* caused an unnecessary sibling rivalry between faith and science. This happened despite the fact that most scientific advancements, like that of Copernicus and Galileo, were encouraged and sponsored by religious institutions. The separation has been exacerbated by the modern error of *scientific elitism*, the belief that science is the only way to know any fact with objective certainty. This error denigrates religion to merely dealing in matters of subjective opinion, not matters of fact.

The truth is, as we have demonstrated above, that science is a subset of faith, not the other way around. Both brothers deal with fact. Science just deals with fact that is limited and therefore provable. Faith deals with fact that is unlimited and therefore cannot be proved nor disproved. Brother science is like football, measurable and time-controlled, and uses the equipment of *proof* and *detached observation*. Brother faith is like baseball, with infinite possibilities and no time constraints, using the equipment of *reason* and *personal relationships*. To ask for proof on a question of faith is like playing baseball with a helmet and shoulder pads. To make religious speculation in science is like playing football with a cap and glove. In both cases, we are using the wrong equipment, asking the wrong questions, and widening the breach of misunderstanding between faith and science.

This dissociation is unfortunate, for faith and science were not designed by God to be at odds with one another. Faith without science is lame, and science without faith is recklessly blind. To avoid conflict, each brother should "play with his own toys," or more specifically, science should deal with finite questions on life, and faith should deal with infinite questions on the meaning of life. Each one, properly understood, can help us to know more about creation and the Creator. Faith and science are brothers in arms, for...

> *Science* deals with finite reality.
> *Faith* deals with infinite reality.

Science deals with proof and evidence in the physical world.
Faith deals with reason and experience, regarding the spiritual world.

> *Science* deals with provable fact.
> *Faith* deals with unprovable fact.

Science studies the natural, impersonally.
Faith responds to the Supernatural, personally.

> *Science* is man controlling nature.
> *Faith* is God controlling man.

Science rests on trust in our senses; an implicit natural faith.
Faith rests on trust in our God; an explicit supernatural faith.

> *Science* teaches about life.
> *Faith* teaches about the meaning of life.

Science reduces wonders to facts.

Faith elevates facts to wonders.

> *Science* deals with matters of the mind.
> *Faith* deals with matters of the heart.

Thought generates action. Standing behind every visible deed is first an invisible idea. Confusion or ignorance battles holy truth in the invisible realm of the mind, before our choices and actions are made. For our minds to understand God and the world as best it can, we need to find the proper intellectual relationship that exists between faith and science. With the conflict resolved, faith can seek understanding in the realm of the metaphysical, and science can search for answers in the realm of the physical. Harmony between these two brothers can deepen our relationship with our Father and improve relationships in the human family. Peace in the family of ideas will bring us peace of mind.

❧

Faith declares what the senses do not see,
but not contrary to what they see. It is above
them, not contrary to them.

BLAISE PASCAL

Comets

*The whole assembly fell silent, and they listened while
Paul and Barnabas described the signs and wonders God
had worked among the Gentiles through them.*

Acts 15:12

On a cool and clear evening in the spring of 1997, my family
stood outside looking up into the twilight sky. A comet was
streaking by the earth. With its tail of vapor streaming brightly
behind it, this rock of ice could be seen by the naked eye. Visible only for a period of time, the comet Halle-Bopp would never
be seen again by my children. In fact, many comets are seen once
and then disappear for millions of years, as they travel on their
eccentric journeys throughout the solar system. "Look carefully
kids," I advised my children. "A phenomenon like this will never
appear again. This will be the last time you will ever see this
comet." My 3 year-old daughter Erin appeared unimpressed by
my words. She responded by saying, "Not for me, Daddy. I will
see this comet again in the Kingdom of God. Then I'm going to
get a ride on the comet!" Erin had reminded me once more that
we must become like a *child*, not an adult, to enter the Kingdom. For in the mystical heart of a child, phenomena of *science*
and *faith* are one and the same.

In the mind of an adult, the continuity and repetition within
nature begin, after many years, to take the wonder out of nature. Phenomena is reduced to fact, mystery is replaced by science. We think we can explain away everything. Yet a sense of
wonder is vital, for without it, we begin to forget about the Cre-

31

ator behind the creation. It is for such faithless moments as these that God will provide a "wake-up call to our heart" by directly entering into nature — disclosing in a supernatural moment a spectacular revelation that cannot be explained in any other way except by using that wondrous word that baffles the skeptics and delights the faithful: *miracle*.

Like a comet appearing brightly in the sky, God streaks across our world. For a moment, the invisible God is revealed visibly, and we can remember the childlike faith we once possessed, and can possess again. We need not witness the miracle ourselves, we need only a reliable and authoritative voice to tell the real-life tale, and our faith can be renewed once more. As G.K. Chesterton reminded us:

The most incredible thing about miracles is that they happen.

Unlike a witch's incantation or a sorcerer's spell which enslaves and imprisons the poor victim they are cast upon, the miracles of God are antidotes from our own deadly poisons, freeing us to be the childlike persons whom God intended us to be when He created us. Christ bringing sight to the blind opens our eyes to see the holiness we had been blinded to. Christ making the deaf hear opens our ears to the sounds of love that had been only silence before. Miracles offer hope, and hope awakens faith, and faith in action becomes love.

But the reality of miracles is not always accepted by modern secular culture. Materialism wedded to a pseudo-scientific mentality has attempted to make miracles an antiquated illusion of the past. They are rejected by either an open denial of the possibility of miracles, or by watering down the definition of miracle so greatly as to eliminate the supernatural element — each effectively denies miracles. In the latter case, we reduce miracles to natural wonders, like the birth of a child or a sunset, which show God working indirectly but never directly. Miracle stories are interpreted as merely metaphors for humanistic charity. Clearly, God does work in natural events, but miracles challenge us to believe that God also works in *super*natural events as well, such as in a virgin being with child or a man rising from the dead. These events have no scientific explanation, but point to the direct intervention of God. Some may still cling to the belief that science will someday explain away these events. Yet not only is this kind of thinking unscientific, it is to have *faith* in some future science that does not yet exist. Miracles such as the virgin birth and the resurrection have defied scientific explanation for 2,000 years, and they will continue to mystify the materialist and delight the faithful for centuries to come.

The former belief, that miracles are simply not possible, implies a *faith* in the absolute constancy of scientific laws. But scientific laws don't control nature, they are merely generalizations taken from observations of how nature works. The Creator of nature is free to add what He wills to nature. Supernatural additions are not contradictions. A God who created natural laws is superior to them. Denying the possibility of miracles also denies a massive amount of reliable witnesses throughout history whose testimony should not be simply ignored.

Christianity is a religion based on a miracle — the miracle of the resurrection. We believe that a dead man, Jesus of Nazareth, rose from the dead. We believe this to be not a symbol, not a myth, not a metaphor, but a *fact*. This fact is our foundation. Take away miracles and we take away Christianity. There are other religions based on ideas and truths, but none based on miracle except Christianity and Judaism. Christianity is not based on "love thy neighbor." That would be mistaking the effect for the cause. People don't get martyred for preaching love — they get put on the "Oprah Winfrey Show." Love is our response to the fact that Jesus is risen. Love follows from faith, our faith in a Miracle Man. Knock down this first miraculous *domino*, and all the other pieces of Christianity will fall as well. "If Christ has not been raised, then empty is… your faith" (1 Cor 15:14). But we can't knock this one down even if we try. And there are scientific demythologizing scholars who do try! The miracle of the risen Christ is bigger than any one of us. Deny it if they must, but they cannot destroy it. Faith in miracles will continue despite those who would reduce them to superstition or illusion. Miracles, a *problem* for the secular world, are a *promise* to us.

Miracles shock our sensibilities when we are most insensible. They bring us back to the foundations of our faith. They remind us, first, of *the sovereignty of God*. For what God has set into motion from the beginning, like sexual procreation, He can bypass if He so chooses, as in the case of Mary and her precious Child. If the repetitions of nature are willed by God to begin with, then our faith in miracles only reasserts our faith in God. Secondly, miracles remind us of *the omnipresence of God*. A miraculous God is not only a God of the past and future, but God in the here and now. His presence is as real and as simple as a child's prayer proclaims. Finally, miracles remind us of the future *glory of God* that we will share. In the resurrection of Jesus and His conquest of death, God has revealed in the past our present hope in a future destiny when all creation will worship the Lord. Every atom will bow to His glory. Every drop of water will genuflect before Him. And every humbled sinner will become an exalted saint.

Jesus *is* the Miracle Man. His birth, life, and death is the greatest miracle of all. He came to walk on water, and teach us how to do some of the things He did, and greater far than these. Jesus came to foretell a Kingdom where my Erin can sail the sky on a comet's tail. The life of every Christian can become the embodiment of these words by Walt Whitman:

"As for me, I know nothing but miracles."

❧

Miracles are signs not to them that believe, but to them that believe not. THOMAS AQUINAS

Tractor Beams

Let no one deceive himself. If anyone among you considers himself wise in this age, let him become a fool so as to become wise. For the wisdom of this world is foolishness in the eyes of God.   1 Corinthians 3:18-19a

In most contemporary science fiction, the spaceships come equipped with what is known as a "tractor beam." It is a fantasy device that allows the ship to latch on to another ship, and hold it in tow. This device was popularized by the television show *Star Trek*. The tractor beam could be utilized any time at the Captain's discretion.

We have a tractor beam as well. It is a *faith tractor beam*. However, whereas the science fiction device was used consciously and occasionally, our device can be triggered "on" unconsciously and continually. It is inevitable that we all use our *faith tractor beam*, it is only a question of how. We were designed to be with God. God designed us with the capacity to relate to Him through faith — the capacity to reconnect with Him. But when we reject God, our tractor beam functions anyway, attaching ourselves to someone or something that will bring us the happiness and control we desire. Blaise Pascal, a French thinker of the 17th century, understood this:

> *It is natural for the mind to believe, and for the will to love; so, failing real objects, they must fix on false ones.*

I have been teaching theology to young teens and adults for a little less than twenty years, and I have *never met an atheist*! Please

35

don't misunderstand this. I have met individuals who claim to be atheists. But practically speaking, they inevitably attach their faith to a "god" that allows them to place themselves up as most important. Show me anyone, and eventually I will find a god they believe in. If it isn't *the* God, the Creator of the universe, it is inevitably someone or something that makes them the object of primary importance in their universe. Life, therefore, consists not of a choice between religion or not religion, but of a choice between true religion or false religion. Everyone practices a religion! If we are not connected to God, we are attaching ourselves to another god.

I once had a student who proclaimed his atheism proudly to the other students in the classroom. He was a bright and reasonably nice kid. I spent some class time allowing him to express his reasons why he had rejected God. I painstakingly tried to show him multiple flaws in his reasoning. I then presented to the class twelve solid arguments for the existence of God. But he refused to accept any of my criticisms, and he denied the validity of every single argument for God. Finally, I grew tired of trying to help him, and concentrated my efforts on the rest of the class. Two weeks later, this same young man came walking into my classroom for that day's session. He noticed that I had placed a bumper sticker on the room's bulletin board. It was an advertisement proclaiming the magical properties of "new age" crystals. It had been given to me earlier in the day as a joke by another student. When the young atheist saw this, his eyes lit up, and a big smile came across his face. "You believe in crystals… So do I!" he exclaimed. "Truthfully, no," I told him, "I think magic crystals are just nonsense." His face fell. He walked silently away, disappointed and a little hurt. He wouldn't believe in a Creator, but he was willing to believe that pieces of shiny rock had enchanting powers. Intellectually, he was an atheist. But spiritually, he was no atheist. He had unwittingly attached his *faith tractor beam* to something that would give him the comfort and security of faith without the loss of personal control and risk. He remained his own god.

Life is the story of man's search for God or god. History is the record of this search. Finding God has brought great joy. Losing God by replacing Him with anything else has brought great sorrow. The tragedy of history has been humanity trying to find something other than God to give them happiness. Our culture places a tremendous amount of time, money, and energy on romance, sexuality, possessions, art, science, and alcohol. These are all good things, each in proper perspective. But if we make any of these our primary concern, misdirecting our *faith tractor beam* at them, they will bring us great sorrow. As C.S. Lewis reminded us, anything that becomes a god becomes a demon. Hidden within secular culture, there are many popular "religions." Among them are three that vex and entrance the human heart and mind.

The romantic religion. Our *faith tractor beam* can easily be unconsciously triggered toward the opposite sex. As solitary individuals on this planet, it is easy to assume that the romantic "other" can fill the emptiness inside ourselves. The phenomenon of physical attraction combined with psychological infatuation make a formidable love potion. If we drink it, we live the illusion that another person can make us happy! We shoulder onto our love partner an immense burden that no human can carry. Only God can. This begins to explain why so many find themselves dissatisfied in their most intimate personal relationships.

The playboy religion. Sex is a multi-billion dollar a year industry, with its scope of influence increasing geometrically in our culture. Much of it is fueled by natural healthy sexual interest turned decadent into lust and addiction, but is also fueled psychologically by those who seek to use sex to dominate another, and with the perception of power, they make themselves into a god. Whereas the romantic religion creates the other into a god, the playboy religion reduces the other into a "pet" to be captured. The conqueror acts as a god while the vanquished is reduced to an object. But casual sex can only remind us of our personal emptiness. When we treat persons like animals, we begin to see ourselves as animals as well. And animals only die. We have not found a cure, we have merely spread the disease.

The drug religion. We have popularized drugs, particularly alcohol, that when abused can temporarily rob us of our humanity. The emptiness we experience can be forgotten by chemically deadening our minds and altering our moods. We long to forget, to escape the burden of humanity. This escape is often a pleasurable sensation, but it is only temporary. The "party night before" gives way to the "morning after." Consciousness returns, harder than ever to face, with the memory of the chemically-induced pleasure remaining attractive and potentially addictive. The freedom drugs offer is addiction, and addiction is slavery. We have not "solved" our personal emptiness, we have only exacerbated it.

These "religions" and others have been around since the Fall of man. They are nothing new. What is new for American culture, however, is how these "religions" have become mainstream. Drug abuse, for example, once an aspect of the counterculture, has become more acceptable in the culture. Sexual promiscuity, once a skeleton in our cultural closet, has come *out*, seen by many as merely an alternative lifestyle. Each of these false "religions" compete for our attention. They are attractive, appealing, and destructive.

Culture is a system of social traditions that provides answers for personal questions. This being true, then secular human culture is anything but secular. Religion has not been removed from secular culture, it has been *concealed* in secular culture. With traditional religion being marginalized by the artistic elite, these "religions" offered are labyrinths leading nowhere except to more alienation and dehumanization. Offering anything material as a way to fill spiritual emptiness is like trying to fill the Grand Canyon with a small bag of marbles. We were made for more. We were made for God.

Christianity is an opportunity for us to become rebels. I am not referring to the mere *form* of rebellion, as done by hypocritical rock stars, but a real *substantive* rebellion against a culture that sells a narcissistic self-centered human utopia. We can declare God before all! We can replace this culture's *man*ifesto with our "*God*ifesto." Attaching our *faith tractor beam* to the infinite God gives us infinite possibilities, free from enticing cultural chains that offer slavery in the name of freedom. We can defy romance, sexual license, drugs, possessions, art, science, money, prestige, success, friendship, marriage... as religion. Nothing above God! God is the only "addiction" that is not addictive. He can set us free. We must abandon it all for the sake of a call. Christian faith is a declaration of independence from earth through an interdependence with heaven. Let the rebellion begin.

❧

Thou hast made us for Thyself. And our hearts are restless, until they rest in Thee.

St. Augustine

Moonlight

They exchanged the truth of God for a lie and revered and worshiped the creature rather than the creator, who is blessed forever.
                                                        Romans 1:25

It was a wonderful evening to watch a sunset. The sky was tinted in reds, oranges, purples and blues. Golden beams of light streaked across the horizon. I was holding my two-year-old daughter Kate in my arms. Despite the panoply of color before her, Kate had her eyes fixed in another direction. She was looking at the moon. The light of the moon, not that of the sun, was what interested Kate. What she couldn't know at that moment was that she was, in fact, looking at the light of the sun. As we know, the moon does not generate light, it merely reflects light that originates from the sun. Kate just assumed that the moon was the source of the light. She gazed at the light that came from the moon, and missed the glory of the light that came from the sun.

Kate's mistake was understandable. We often make a similar mistake ourselves. Whereas Kate did not understand the physics of light, we misunderstand the metaphysics of God's light. We can all mistakenly become so enamored of *something* or *someone* in creation that we ignore or forget the *Someone*, God, who is the Creator of creation. Just as my Kate stared at the moonlight and missed the light of the *sun* in the sky, we can become dazzled by the lights of the world, and miss the light of the *Son* of God.

As Christians, we are prepared to resist the lure of evil. That is fundamental to developing an authentic morality. But the truth is that we also have to resist the lure of good, placing too much value on anything or anyone in the created world which distracts us from God. Good can become a subtle evil. A realization of this fact is fundamental to developing an authentic spirituality. C.S. Lewis, a Christian writer and apologist, explained this profound truth in an essay entitled *The Weight of Glory*.

> *The books or the music in which we thought the beauty was located will betray us if we trust them; it was not in them, it only came through them, and what came through them was longing. These things — the beauty, the memory of our own past — are good images of what we really desire; but if they are mistaken for the thing itself, they turn into dumb idols, breaking the hearts of their worshipers. For they are only the scent of a flower we have not yet found, the echo of a tune we have not yet heard, news from a country we have never visited.*

Lewis is articulating a profound insight gained after much reflection on how we all experience the world. To fully appreciate it requires each of us to reflect on our own experiences as well. Why does a particular song, a scene in a movie, a past memory, or a particular place, move us so profoundly? C.S. Lewis is telling us that each of these things is like a directional beacon pointing heavenward. God is working through them. In our encounter with these things or persons, we experience a sense of longing for something far beyond the thing or person. When we long to hear "that" song again, it isn't the song that we love, it's the sensation of longing for something or Someone beyond it that the song stirs within us — that is what we really love. The *something* is heaven. The *Someone* is God.

Whenever we hold on to any good in this world, without remembering the source of the joy that we derive from the good, we take it out of its proper perspective. Whether we are aware of it or not, we have made an idol. This idolatry is *lunacy*, which ironically is taken from the word *lunar*, referring to the moon. The "moonlight" of this world can make us forget the "sunlight" of heaven that the moon reflects. My Kate is not alone in her confusion. Thousands of years ago the Greeks understood how easily the sun and moon could be confused. In their mythology, they imagined the sun god Apollo and the moon god Artemis as twins. They saw that it was easy to get twins confused. In the making of idols, we perpetuate a similar spiritual confusion.

It is a kind of idolatry, for example, when a person chooses to "live in the past." As we get older, we can create in our minds a picture of the past that has more significance than the events ever had for us when we were originally experiencing them. We long to return to the "simple days" of childhood, forgetting how hard it was to learn how to tie our shoes! Personally, I'm still working on the double knot. Rose-colored glasses can create an image of past events that is heavenly — and therein lies the flaw. Only heaven is truly heavenly. Memories can point to heaven, however they do not contain it.

Idolatry can be extended to social and religious movements as well. We see this in nature-worship that prescribes being "one with nature" as the spiritual antidote for all our modern ills. But it is not logical for us who have a supernatural destiny to worship the natural. That is looking for God below us, rather than above. Worship of the mischievous nature god, *Pan*, can only lead to *pan*ic. For Christians, the love of nature needs to be tempered by the love of God who shines through it. Nature, as St. Francis of Assisi understood it, is not our mother but our sister. The natural universe is like a prism that takes the light of God and reflects a variety of colors. The colors point to one light behind the prism. Just as moonlight is reflected sunlight, nature is reflected *Son*light.

Even our most "sacred" of human relationships can become idolatrous. Consider the experience of marital love. The love a husband receives from his wife did not originate in his wife. His wife is love's instrument. God is love's source. For the husband to accept his wife's love, and then to reject God, is to have inadvertently rejected his wife as well. He has cut himself off from the source that feeds the stream of her love. He has taken the beautiful gift of marital love, and made it an idol, rather than hearing in marital love an echo of the far greater love that flows from God.

Memories fade. Earthly romance wanes. Diamonds are not forever. Rock and roll, despite the words of its promoters, will die. Cities will turn to dust and rust. Stars will burn out. But God lives forever. With His grace, we will as well. The key to doing so lies in a simple song I sing to Kate under the moonlight at bedtime. The words are from Jesus.

Seek ye first the Kingdom of God, and His righteousness.
And all these things shall be added unto you. Alleluia.

These words offer proper spiritual perspective. Trust in the Lord above all. Deify only the Deity. When I forget this truth, I will hold my little Kate close to me, look to the sky, and let the moonlight remind me.

And you and I have need of the strongest spell that can be found to wake us from the evil enchantment of worldliness which has been laid upon us for nearly a hundred years.
C.S. LEWIS

Starship Enterprise

Do not be conformed to this world but be transformed....
Romans 12:2a (RSV - Catholic Ed.)

In my childhood, I used to lie on the couch, potato chips at hand, and watch the Starship Enterprise warp through the universe. *Star Trek* was one of many television shows I chose to watch over reading a book or healthy outdoor exercise. The ship and Captain Kirk were the embodiment of my male fantasy — never wearing a tie, a big-screen TV at the front of the ship's bridge, traveling to strange new places, accumulating frequent flyer miles, attractive female crew members at the Captain's beck and call, and most importantly, flying through space. *Star Trek* captured my imagination, a fantastic voyage to where no man had gone before. I had assumed that when I reached adulthood, these fantasies would be left behind. But in a way I never imagined, the fantasy has come true.

The central problem facing the West today is spiritual homelessness. This is not to be confused with physical houselessness — the problem of finding shelter for people in poverty. Homelessness is a problem every person on Earth has. As G.K. Chesterton discovered, earth is a place where we feel homeless at home. The world has its wonders, but it is far from perfect. None of us is perfectly comfortable here. We experience things that our spirit fights to overcome, such as disease, aging, sin, evil, and death. We were not meant for such a world as this. Consider our frustration with the phenomena of *time*, *love*, and *happiness*.

44

Time. At night, I often sneak into my children's bedrooms and quietly watch them sleep. Looking at their angelic faces, a wave of love comes over me. I want this moment to last forever, but it never does. Night passes, morning comes, and I forget. It seems as though I am in a constant battle with time. I want these profound transcendent moments to remain, but they come and go like the days. Everyone has experiences like these, yet we can't hold on to them or have enough of them. Time is an enemy. We battle the man-made clock throughout the day, and nature's clock throughout the years. No other animal species exhibits our frustration with time. Never enough time to talk, never enough time to laugh, never enough time to love. Perhaps we were not meant for time, perhaps we are meant for eternity.

Love. Gazing at my sleeping children also provides another illustration of the inadequacy of this world. I experience a love for my children that is deeper and more intense than any love I have ever known. And yet I still fail in my attempt to love them. Instead of love, there are moments when I give them my smallness, my impatience, my anger. Why can't I love them perfectly? I desire to love them more purely, but I cannot will it. Is anyone capable of perfect love? Is there a "place" of perfect love that matches this longing I have? We have all felt inadequate in the love we have given, and embarrassed by the love we have received. Trapped in an earthly world of sin, our love suffers its effect. Yet we still long for a love that is heavenly. Our longing for perfect love points to heaven — the "world" of perfect love.

Happiness. Most of us have experienced dissatisfaction with time and love. But our experience of happiness, though more subtle, contains frustration as well. In our moments of greatest joy — going to the prom, graduation, wedding days, birth of children, etc. — as great as they were, we still long for more. We never seem to reach the limit to our longing for joy. Nothing in this world fully satisfies. Like a hunger seeking food, like insatiable thirst seeking water, our longing for joy beyond human limits points to the fact that we were created for *boundless joy* — a supernatural joy that this world cannot completely offer.

Earth is not home. What we love about earth is that it gives us glimpses of our true home. Just as a shadow darkly reflects a figure that is more concrete than it, earth is a shadow that reflects a world that is more concrete as well. C.S. Lewis, a Christian writer and apologist, noted this when he described our world as "the shadowlands." The reality of heaven will make earth seem unreal. We are "ghosts" here on earth, we will become real in heaven. Lewis illustrates this when describing the destruction of the fictional world of Narnia. He takes this profound adult insight and describes it with the simplicity of a child.

> *When Aslan said you could never go back to Narnia, he meant the Narnia you were thinking of. But that was not the real Narnia. That had a beginning and an end. It was only a shadow or a copy of the real Narnia, which has always been here and always will be here…And of course it is different; as different as a real thing is from a shadow or as waking life is from a dream.*

If Earth is not home, then what is it? Earth is a starship, traveling through outer space. It is a ship that has many of the comforts we desire but not all that we need. It is so well equipped that frequently we mistake it for home.* Heaven, our eternal destination of joy, is home. Heaven is the "undiscovered country." Like the American pioneers drawn to the west, heaven acts like a magnet, pulling us towards our true destiny — to live in eternity without time, love without limit, joy without sorrow, dawn without darkness.

To reach this ultimate destination, while on our fantastic voyage, we must relinquish the Captain's chair to the Captain.

---

* From *Turning Back the Clock*, Peter Kreeft, Ignatius Press, 1994.

He built this ship, He powers this ship, and only He can bring us home. Our task, in the language of *Star Trek*, is...

> *Heaven: the final frontier.*
> *These are the voyages of the Starship Earth.*
> *Its mission: to explore strange new spiritual worlds,*
> > *to seek out eternal life and new civilizations —*
> > > *the City of God,*
> > *to boldly go where we have never gone*
> > > *before — Heaven.*

Earth is like the Starship Enterprise, commanded by Jesus Christ, moving through time and space towards an eternal destiny. Christians, His Starfleet crew, are in His service. We are obedient to Him and loyal to His chain of command, confident that Christ will bring us through any barrier and lead us home, where we will live long and prosper.

❧

If I find in myself a desire which no experience in this world can satisfy, the most probable explanation is that I was made for another world.

C.S. LEWIS

The Mountain

Rejoice always, never cease praying, render constant thanks; such is God's will for you in Christ Jesus.

1 Thessalonians 5:17

On the mountain of Sinai, Moses spoke to God face to face.
On the mountain of Zion, David built God's holy city.
On the mountain of Carmel, Elijah listened and obeyed God.
On the mountain near Bethsaida, Jesus prayed in solitude.
On the mountain, we will encounter God.

Prayer is not an option. Prayer is essential to the Christian life. We must ascend the heights of holiness, we must go to the mountain, we must pray.

Prayer is an invitation to a confrontation. Consequently, like mountain climbing, its dangers are commonly avoided. It is far more convenient for us to keep God as an intellectual exercise. We talk *about* God rather than *to* Him. We stay on safe, common ground by asking ourselves, "Am I comfortable in my relationship with God?" And we respond with a satisfied "Yes." Distance gives us comfort. But there are two persons in every relationship. The health of the relationship should not be judged by whether we are comfortable with God, but rather by whether God is comfortable with us. That is why communication is needed in any relationship, to learn the truth. Prayer is first contact. Prayer is personal, and personal contact creates a level of intimacy and risk. Intimacy robs us of comfort and makes us grow. Defenses must be let down, intellect must be checked, and the heart must lead. Mountain climbing can be dangerous, but the rewards are great. A new universe, a new covenant, a new life begins with the first word uttered by our heart to our Creator. Prayer is the heart moving to higher ground, to holy ground.

On our climb to the mountaintop, we continue to confront the choice to pray or not to pray. In that decision, the battle between heaven and hell rages inside us. It is a struggle of infinite significance. Ignore the choice to pray and the choice is made. Evade the choice and the choice is done. Prayer or power? What will animate us through life? As we contemplate the decision, faith and doubt wage war. Doubt tells us that prayer is just too common, too trite, too hard, too traditional, too mundane, too passive, too uncertain, too simplistic, too boring, too old-fashioned for the modern age. But faith battles back. The truth is that without prayer, God remains dark and distant — a Jericho mile away. Our excuses reveal flaws in *us*, not in prayer. Prayer is too revealing, too awesome, too humbling, and too powerful. It's a spectacle far greater than any sought by world travelers and thrill seekers. Prayer is the point where man meets God, where the sea meets the sky, where earth meets heaven. Prayer is the beginning of solitude in our relationship with God and the end of solitary us. As Jacob wrestled with God, God will wrestle with us, for He desires loving conquest. We are to die, to be reborn into dazzling, radiant, resurrected beings who can live forever with the God who made us. There is no greater journey, no greater experience. Prayer is a transcendent voyage to heaven's gate. The moment we begin is the triumph of angels over devils, the marriage of God and mankind — for only through prayer will man learn to *be* kind.

During our climb to God, it is easy to avoid prayer by altering the very nature of prayer, converting prayer into a monologue of mental wanderings or a one-sided list of demands. We need to remind ourselves continually what prayer is. Like love, prayer is known only by doing. Words can, however, guide...

For prayer is not knowing about God,
prayer is knowing God.
For prayer is not talking at God,
prayer is talking to God.
For prayer is not taking time for God,
prayer is making time with God.
For prayer is not just talking,
prayer is also listening.
For prayer is not about making us feel better,
prayer is about making us better.
For prayer is not about changing God,
prayer is about changing ourselves.
For prayer is not a relationship with a person,
prayer is a relationship with the Person.
For prayer is not getting what we want from God,
prayer is God getting what He wants from us.

As we ascend the heights of holiness, we begin as all relationships begin, with a surge of the heart. As we speak our words, our soul disengages from matter and we build a relationship with Christ. Mountain climbing calls for a repetition of the fundamentals. For our prayer life to remain vital, we need to include four basic phrases that lie at the heart of any good relationship.

I'm sorry. Words of contrition reveal ourselves as we truly are, for humility is the foundation of prayer. This is not a relationship between equals. We stand for our president, but we kneel before our God. The truth is that God is always faithful to His relationship with us, but we are not always faithful to Him. Recognition of sin is necessary for us to know the truth about ourselves. And if we live truly, we can relate to God more honestly. Words that are not true cannot pass from earth to heaven. This is the first step on the mountain of prayer. But we should not remain here. We need to move through fault and on to forgiveness.

Thank you. Words of thanksgiving remind us that this is not a relationship between equals. Even though we can be credited for being instruments of goodness, we should give credit to the Source of all that is good, of all that is. All our gifts flow from God the Giftgiver. The more thanks that are given, the more an attitude of gratitude is received.

Please. Our words of petition should be predicated with "Thy will be done," thereby conforming our will to His. We can be confident that God will answer all our prayers. We cannot be confident that He will answer them according to our designs. His answer may be "No." A request ought to be followed by an attitude of watchfulness, listening and waiting for God to respond in His own way.

I love you. Words of adoration speak to the very nature of God Himself. In love, we have prayerfully reached the mountain's zenith. In loving God, we experience our restless heart at rest, and we discover the biggest surprise of all. Just as our heart has longed to encounter God, God has been yearning for us to encounter Him. Our *El Shaddai,* our "God of the Mountain" has waited for us to reach Him — the joy is mutual.

The Father has even given us the Son, to teach us how to pray. Jesus will climb with us. He will show us how. The Gospels show that Jesus prayed constantly: in surrender, in solitude, in thanksgiving, in humility. Jesus always prayed *before* important decisions and events. He used the prayer traditions of His time. As illustrated in the Lord's Prayer, Jesus prayed in a simple, direct, and intimate way. He invites us to call God, as He did, our *Abba* — our Papa, our Daddy — to live in filial sonship with the Father. With Jesus the Son at our side, we can climb the mountain to God the Father. Loving the Father as the Son instills the Holy Spirit. The Spirit *is* the love between the Father and the Son. It is He who will propel us heavenwards. Like mountain climbing, prayer is a dynamic activity, for when we pray, we involve ourselves in the Trinitarian life of God. We climb *to* God, *with* God, and *by* God.

God, be my Father and I will be your Son.
Jesus, be my Brother and I will be your Friend.
Spirit of both, be within me and I will be your Love.

In prayer, we transcend the limits of humanity and ascend to the unlimited divinity. We cannot remain on common ground. We are destined for a meeting on holy ground. Our "God of the Mountain" will provide fresh air that will clear our heads and a fresh view that will inspire our hearts. The best kind of prayer is the one that we are doing. The Mountain of God will be safe haven from the valley of death. We can delay no longer. Just do it.

Though my body may walk in the valley,
my spirit can take to the mountain.

❧

To stand on one leg and prove God's existence is a
very different thing from going down on
one's knees and thanking Him.

SOREN KIERKEGAARD

The Field

> *"What eye has not seen, and ear has not heard, and what has not entered the human heart, what God has prepared for those who love him," this God has revealed to us through the Spirit.*   1 Corinthians 2:9-10a

> *If you build it, he will come.*   — the Voice

Like Elijah hearing the voice of God in a whispering sound, Ray Kinsella, in the 1989 film *Field of Dreams*, hears "the voice" in his cornfield. This is not as fantastic as we might think. Jesus chose many secular images in His parables on the Kingdom of God to illustrate a similar truth: God is encountered in real life — in a farmer's field, at a wedding feast, with a shepherd and his flock, or in a relationship between an estranged father and son. In each, the ordinary reveals the extraordinary God. In *Field of Dreams*, Ray Kinsella is a modern-day Noah, led by a mysterious voice to build a baseball field where he and others can be healed of their deepest pain. Looking at this film for a moment, as a tool of theology, seeing "the voice" as God, the baseball field can be seen as an extension of God's Kingdom — a nexus point between heaven and earth. Is it possible that heaven could interface with earth? It is more than possible, it is actual. Looking at the Christian view of heaven from a horizontal, human perspective, heaven is the place where dreams come true! Not our selfish dreams that make us feel better, but those good dreams that make us better. Our dreams are found only after they have been lost, subsumed into the will of God. Seen from this perspective, heaven is being who we are meant to be, united with those we love, doing what we love, fulfilling our true destiny through the perfect will of God. Using images rather than ideas to understand heaven, heaven is a state of being where we reconcile with others to bring all into family and friendship, play baseball with Shoeless Joe Jackson, paint with Michelangelo, study theology with Thomas Aquinas, or discuss law with Abraham Lincoln.

It's so beautiful here. For me, it's like a dream come true.
John Kinsella

These images, though limited and humanistic, serve an important purpose. We need images that show heaven as a real place, where we have a concrete existence and a resurrected body. We will be more real in heaven than we are on earth. The risen Christ could walk through walls, not because *He* was transparent, but because *the walls* were transparent in comparison to Him. Jesus walking through walls would be like us walking through fog. Earth is the land of shadows, not heaven. As a circle is to a sphere, this world is to the Kingdom of heaven.

Oh yes (there is a heaven.) It's the place where dreams come true.
John Kinsella

Having been a teacher for close to two decades, most resistance to the good news about the Kingdom of God lies not in it being unreasonable, but in it being unimaginable. Many youth in America can grasp the idea, they just cannot believe the image. Their imaginations have been so darkened that they cannot believe the world is as wonderful as Christianity proclaims it to be. Often they are more motivated by not wanting to be in hell than aspiring to be in heaven. Hell, they can imagine. Heaven, they dare not hope to imagine. Deep inside, they can only hope that *some* of what Christianity proclaims is true. They will "settle" for some concept of an afterlife and hopefully a benevolent Creator. But a Father who loves them beyond their wildest dreams; that is hard to believe. And so weak "play-it-safe" dreams translate into a halfhearted faith and a half-lived existence.

For it's money they have, but peace they lack.

Terrance Mann

The imagination of many secular Christians regarding heaven is often more Hindu than it is Christian. In general, we can identify two contrasting views of heaven among world religions. In the Hindu understanding of *nirvana*, heaven is seen as "the extinguishing of the flame." Heaven is a state of non-being where we become less than what we were on earth, but that "lessening" is a good experience. Like a candle blown out by the wind, our individuality will merge into the great consciousness of God. This is seen as a good because Hindus identify selfhood as the source of misery and illusion. Human beings are released into God, who is not a person, but rather ultimate reality. In the afterlife, each person is like a drop of water entering the great ocean of God.

In the Christian understanding of the *Kingdom of God*, heaven is seen as the "prodigal son returning to the Father." Heaven is a state of being where we become more than what we were on earth, and this "purifying" is a good experience. Like an eternal flame, our individuality will be made perfect by our loving Father. This is seen as a good because we identify sin as the source of misery and illusion. Human beings are fulfilled in the beatific vision of God, who is the ultimate three-Personal God. In the afterlife, each person is like a sojourner whose travels bring him from home to *Home*, from pain to *Paradise*.

I could've sworn this was Heaven.

John Kinsella

These are brief summaries of the Hindu and Christian notions of the afterlife. I will leave the more precise analysis to the scholars. Nor do we need debate the relative merits of the two concepts of the afterlife. What the mind cannot resolve, the heart can. *If* the bodily resurrection of Jesus is true, then so is our claim for a personal eternal afterlife. For Easter is not merely the celebration of Jesus' transfiguration into a resurrected being; it is the celebration that we can share in the resurrection, for He is the Way! Having surrendered control of our soul over to Christ, He will guide us through our "cross-training," and in death we will be what we were intended to be by God — a resurrected union of body and soul, with our sinful self destroyed by the awesome power of Christ.

> *Go the distance.*   the Voice

As we confront the reality of heaven and hell while still on earth, still trapped in the deception of sin, we must be on guard. Reality can differ greatly from our image of it. Hell, from the vantage point of sinful human existence, appears attractive. Evil's nature is to lie, to appear its opposite. Hell is the place where we proclaim: "My will be done!" Hell is placing ourselves up as god. Pride is attractive, lust is enticing, greed is addictive. Sinning appears "fun" — that's why we do it. Some will prefer to rule in Hell than serve in heaven. Hell's charm lies in its not desiring us to become any more than we are. Hell requires nothing; only those that desire to laziness need apply.

> *Son, if I had only been a doctor for five minutes, now that would have been a tragedy.*
>   Doc "Moonlight" Graham

Heaven, in contrast, will appear difficult and challenging. God is Truth, therefore, He will not "lower the bar" of expectations for His beloved children. Heaven is the place where we proclaim: "God's will be done!" Heaven is acknowledging God as God. Humility will exalt, service will heal, suffering will be transformed to joy. Sin will be no more. Heaven's choir will accept the Father's love and renounce self-centered slavery. Heaven's lure lies in God's desiring us to be more than what we are now. Heaven requires transformation; only those that aspire to goodness need apply.

> *Is that why you did this? For you? I think you better stay*
> *here, Ray.*
> Shoeless Joe

Emphasis on heaven has been criticized as the opiate of earth, but it serves just the opposite purpose. Our vision heavenward places an infinite value on all that is earthbound. The Christian task is not merely to bring man into heaven, but also heaven into man. We can begin the Kingdom on earth. To accomplish this, we need to keep our eyes on the prize and look heavenward. Because it is difficult to describe heaven conceptually, we can vision our heavenly destiny in terms of metaphor and paradox. To enter the Kingdom, "put on" the imagination of a child, and *the Kingdom* becomes...

A land where
  life is celestial laughter and forever fun
  prodigal sons return and wayward daughters find rest
  absent fathers attend to mend and unfit mothers are
    capable
  abandoned children are secure and the unborn have names

A land where
  stars wish upon us
  forgiveness falls like rain
  beauty is found in every beast
  lost causes are won
  chocolate is nutritious

singers sing colors but never the blues
purity is pleasure
law is liberty
justice is service
kindness is courage
humility is nobility
fear is forgotten
charity is cherished
fidelity is forever.

A land where
   we shall see our God face to face, secure in His arms
   reunite with our best friend from Nazareth
   behold the beatific vision of God
   be forever Home.

If you insist on having your own way, you will get it.
Hell is the enjoyment of your own way forever.
If you really want God's way with you,
      you will get it in Heaven.

DANTE ALIGHIERI

Part Two:

THE HORIZONTAL CROSSBEAM
The Mystery of Humanity and Our Relationship to Others

THE WAY OF LOVE

Title	*Theme*
1. The Gift	Nature of Love
2. The Ring	Sex and Marriage
3. Coke	Marriage and Love
4. Shield	Family
5. Horton the Elephant	Abortion
6. Gravity	Morality
7. Black	Nature of Evil
8. Toys	Possessions
9. The Monster	Art
10. Eden	Drug Abuse
11. Aliens	Nature of Mankind
12. Robin Hood	Personhood

The Gift

So faith, hope, love remain, these three; but the greatest
of these is love.　　　　1 Corinthians 13:13

I sat there on Christmas Eve, staring intently at a present under the tree with my name on it. The room was dark, lit only by the twinkling lights of the Christmas tree. What could it be? A new G.I Joe? New Viewmaster slides? A new Matchbox car? Despite a tremendous amount of energy that I concentrated on the gift, it remained an unfathomable mystery. I could only see it from the outside, from a distance, but I hoped it was something good. Sleep did not come easily that Christmas Eve night. I lay awake in bed, starring at a clock whose hands moved painfully slow. Finally, Christmas morning arrived. I could have the gift as my own. I tore off the wrapping paper to see my gift from the inside out. Mystery gave way to familiarity, familiarity to play. The mystery was solved, my confusion gone, and the fun began.

Love is God's greatest gift. But if it remains distant, unwrapped, seen only from the outside, it is a gift hard to understand. Love is different words in every language, but in deeds it's the same in any language. It is everything to Christians and nothing to tennis players. It is celebrated and misunderstood. Like a child staring at a wrapped Christmas gift, love can be an unfathomable mystery. Philosophers wax about it. Singers croon it. Poets lament it. Capitalists market it. Hollywood exploits it. Evolutionary biologists analyze it. Kings demand it. Performers crave it. Demons fear it. Stoics ignore it. Skeptics deny it. Psy-

61

chiatrists prescribe it. Geneticists identify it. Historians record it. Novelists depict it. Artists illustrate it. Parsons preach it. Playboys diminish it. Movies plot it. Cynics mock it. Governments tax it. Politicians showcase it. Nobility refines it. Children need it. But the mystery of it is best understood by saints from the inside, for only when it is unwrapped and used is it ever understood. Saints live it... because God is it.

We can begin to understand love only by loving. But unlike the material gifts under my Christmas tree, God's gift of love is infinite. We never fully "solve" the mystery of love, we can only be drawn deeper into it, where love begins to "solve" us. Love is an infinite voyage, but though we can't know everything about love, we can know *something*. If we don't try, love becomes either meaningless or, at worst, dangerous. So we can add one more category to the above list: "Teachers explain it." Allow me to rush in where angels never fear to tread, and offer a classic definition: *Love is to will the good of another.* It is a choice to dedicate ourselves to another individual's spiritual growth. To explore this in greater depth, we can examine some basic insights about what love is, and what it is not.

Love is volitional, not emotional. Restated more simply, love is a decision, not a feeling. Despite millions of popular songs to the contrary, love is not a feeling. It is a choice. Feelings, by nature, are temporary, and they are largely dictated by circumstances. They come *to* us, not *from* us. But how we respond to feelings and circumstance is something chosen by us — our attitude. That comes *from* us, not *to* us. We are free to choose to use the gift or not. Feelings can be a part of our decision to love, but love is not dependent on them. If fact, love's true test is when we love someone even though the feeling of love is lacking. We can't "fall in" love; that is a feeling. But we can "rise to" love; that is a decision.

Love is an action, not an intention. Love is an act of the will. The *will* is *desire + resolute action.* We can desire something but never act on it. To will something means to do it! Love is not a noun, it is an action verb! Love is something we do, not dream about. Love is concrete and real, not abstract and mental. Love is active, not passive. It is hard work directed towards another person's well being. It demands of us patience, attentive listening, perseverance, understanding, compassion, honesty, respect, to name a few. Love requires personal sacrifice, and sacrifice is painful. Love's purpose is not to make a person feel better, but rather to make him be better. Love is faith translated into action. To be loving is to be faithful.

Love is a commitment, not a mood. Love comes from God and God is eternal. Therefore love is not limited by time, it is not a passing fancy that starts in a day and ends in a day. If someone claims to love one day, and then not the next, they never loved in the first place. Commitment stands the test of time. "Liking" fluctuates while "love" is constant. "Liking" is dependent on circumstance. "Loving" is independent of circumstances. Every year in the classroom, I ask my students, "Do you love pizza?" Usually one or two will exclaim, "Yes!" "Really," I respond, "would you eat a pizza if it were covered with ants?" Fortunately, I have not yet heard an affirmative response to this challenge. "Then, you don't love pizza, you like it," I explained. "Love is a commitment to a person for better or worse. If the pizza is 'for worse,' throw it out. If your wife turns 'for worse,' stick it out." The point I was teaching my students was that we like something *because*; we love someone *although*. Love is not blind, it is bound. It is not ignoring a person's faults, it is remaining committed to helping them grow despite those faults. We are not required to *like* our neighbor, only to *love* them.

Love is specific, not general. Because love is a concrete action, claims of "loving humanity" or "loving the planet" are meaningless. Jesus understood this, for He did not require us to love humanity in general, He commanded us to love all our neighbors — meaning specific individuals. "Humanity" will not ask a parent for a ride to baseball practice, but a child will. "Humanity" will not inconvenience us on a Saturday afternoon, but visiting an elderly man will. "Loving humanity" is easy, but loving our neighbor, which is real love, is hard.

Love is a paradox, not a parasite. Love appears to some as a contradiction to be avoided. "If I give my heart away," they reason, "I lose my heart. If I love, I risk a broken heart." They believe that love eats away our happiness. But love is not a parasite, it is a paradox. Love will not break our hearts, it can only *make* our hearts. We see this in nature. Put steel through fire and the steel gets stronger, not weaker. A vine needs to be severely pruned if it is to bear new grapes in abundance next season. An apple tree loses its fruit in the fall so that it can produce fresh fruit in the coming year. The caterpillar "dies" in its cocoon in order to rise again as a butterfly. We are no different. This is simply the working principle of life. We must give in order to receive. There is no alternative to this except self-centered death. This is who we are. We love in order to grow.

I never fully grasped this paradox until April 17, 1990. On that day, my gift from God was opened, and I held my child for the first time. She weighed only a few pounds but she weighed heavy on my soul. She melted my heart and for the first time I found it. On that day, I said "good-bye" to my freedom and said "hello" to my baby daughter. I replaced my dreams with hers. I became a father.

These five statements on what love is and what it is not can help us identify real love when we receive it or when we act lovingly ourselves. Not only will love bring us closer to others, it will bring us to God. God is love. The Scriptures do not reveal that God is beauty, joy, happiness, faith, hope, peace, or reason. They reveal that God is love. It is His very nature. The persons of the Father, Son, and Holy Spirit exist in a union of divine love. God's creation is simply an expression of His love. The Father's ultimate act of love was a Christmas gift wrapped in

swaddling clothes, lying in a manger. When we open our hearts
to Christ's love, we connect to God's very nature. By loving God
our Father we become more like Jesus our Brother, and we show
that we belong in God's family. Only when people learn to love
will our war-torn, sorrow-filled, tear-stained human family find
peace. Love is the only gift we can keep by giving it away. Love
is the greatest gift of all — God's gift of Himself. The gift does
not so much place God in our hearts as it places us in the heart
of God.

> *Love is the gift of life,*
> *in a land where clouds rain,*
> *and sorrow remains.*
>
> *Love is the gift of passage,*
> *to the land where God reigns,*
> *and only love remains.*

🍃

Love is the measure by which we all shall be judged.

ST. JOHN OF THE CROSS

The Ring

*Thus they are no longer two but one flesh. Therefore, let
no man separate what God has joined.*   Matthew 19:6

*"Cinderella, you may go to the ball,
but... the magic will end by midnight."*
*"Pandora, you may have a box that contains all evil,
but... do not open it."*

Goodness rests on a provision. Joy is conditional. Violate
the condition and we destroy the joy. Fairy tales of old understood this truth and expressed it through their stories. In
Cinderella, the fairy godmother grants a humble girl a wonderful gift, but she included a midnight time limitation as well.
Although Cinderella didn't fully understand the purpose of the
stipulation, she accepted it and obeyed. As it turns out, because
she left the ball so suddenly at midnight, the prince's longing
for Cinderella only increased and he was almost driven to pursue her. The condition placed on Cinderella's gift actually re-
sulted in enhancing her joy. This is also true of the gifts that our
God-Father bestows upon us, for what is central to ethics is also
central to fairy tales. To cite a few examples in fairy tale style:

*"Women, I will give you the gift of motherhood,
but... do not destroy the child."*
*"Adults, I will give you the gift of alcohol,
but... do not abuse it."*

The Ring

Since evil results from the abuse of good, a moral restriction is necessary to keep good from becoming evil, help from becoming harm, and blessing from becoming curse. God gives gifts with strings attached that enhance the essential joy of the gift.

This is maybe especially true of the gift of sexuality. God's gift of sexuality is given with a string attached, and the string is a *ring*. The essential goodness of sexual intercourse is preserved in the context of marriage. Marriage is the total union of a man and woman with God, symbolized by the wedding ring. As G.K. Chesterton said, sex is an instinct that produces an institution — marriage and family. Marital love is the condition that preserves and enhances sexual joy.

"Men and women, I will give you the joy and beauty of sexual expression,
***but...** no sexual intercourse outside of marriage."*

No moral condition is attacked more often in our modern secular culture than the belief that sex is only for marriage. The modern mentality has run rings around traditional sexual morals. They attack the foundation of sexual morality by saying that sex is not a moral issue at all. Sex is *equal to* pleasure. The Catholic Church, lost in the sexual "dark ages," has mistakenly categorized it as moral, and this mistake has led to much sexual repression. All forms of sexual expression are moral provided there is adult consent. Sex, they believe, is contractual. Mutual consent makes a contract valid, therefore consent makes sex valid.

But let's extend this argument to its logical conclusion. If sex is *not* a moral issue, then by inference, acts involving self-abuse, homosexuality, incest, sadomasochism, transsexuality, bisexuality, transvestitism and bestiality would not be immoral as long as those involve give their consent. Thankfully, most reasonable moral people would reject this conclusion. Most people will "draw the line" somewhere. But if we "draw a line," that assumes there is a moral line to be drawn which makes one act moral and another act immoral. Then sex *is* a moral issue! Human choice alone does not determine what is morally acceptable. God has a will and an intention behind the act of sexual intercourse apart from what we might want it to mean.

Many educators, journalists, actors, and politicians would say that the moral ingredient necessary for an act of sex to be moral is *love*. Sex, they believe, is *equal to* love. But love could be invoked in any of the scenarios listed above. Love alone does not make sex moral — a particular kind of love, *marital love* makes sex moral. The problem in using the term *love* is that it can be applied to hundreds of different dynamics. Brotherly love, friendship love, familial love, romantic love, humanitarian love, and unconditional love are all easily confused. Love is also mistaken for affection or infatuation, which creates even more confusion. We can end the confusion by recommitting ourselves to the fusion of sex and marriage. Sex is for marriage and marriage is for Christ. As this editorial cartoon illustrates, sex in marriage has a nice ring to it:

Teen Grandson: "Gee, Grandad, your generation didn't have all these social diseases. What did you wear to have safe sex?"
Grandad: "A wedding ring."

The modern intellectual divorce that has occurred between sex and marriage is thankfully not permanent. When examining the issue of premarital sex from a Christian point of view, we can consider it from four different perspectives.

*Consider **Jesus**.* Jesus promotes the traditional concept of sex and marriage, so must we. There, that was easy. Please notice that I didn't rely on my authority. I'm just a teacher and a writer. I relied on Jesus' authority. He is the Son of God; we are

68

not. Jesus is *The Word* on the subject. *The Ultimate* is the ultimate authority. In Matthew 19 Jesus raises the traditional marriage to the level of sacrament, by expressing God's divine intention for men and women to marry. And in 1 Corinthians 6, the apostle Paul, filled with the Spirit of the risen Christ, specifically condemns fornication. To question this teaching is to really question Jesus. Jesus is the *Lord of the Ring*. Sex in marriage ought to be hobbit-forming (Sorry — couldn't help it).

Consider the **Pope**. When the pope speaks, he does not speak for himself, but rather for the entire Roman Catholic Church. The word *catholic* means universal. Two thousand years of consistent teaching on sex in marriage is an authority to be considered. This voice from the past and present is joined by other religious traditions such as Eastern Orthodox, Anglican, Lutheran, Methodist, Southern Baptist, Orthodox Judaism, Sunni Moslem, etc. One of my great frustrations in teaching, besides the pay, is meeting young students who see themselves as a *minority* if they believe in reserving sex for marriage. Yet the truth is that they are in the *majority* of human history. Countless legions stand together. Even in our own country, much of mainstream America supports chastity. Hollywood will tell us otherwise, but they lie to make money. They are more interested in generating dollars and cents than common sense.

The Roman Catholic tradition upholds two main purposes to sex. The *unitive purpose*: sex should communicate marital love, and the *procreative purpose*: sex should be open to creating new life. Both need to be present in the relationship in order for the act to be moral. Sex should definitely be enjoyed, just not to the extent of violating the nature of the act — expressing love and creating life.

Consider the **beloved**. Our actions can deceive as well as our words. The fact is that sexual intercourse is full physical union, one of the most intimate things two human beings can do. There is a vulnerability to sexual intimacy. All the more reason not to lie to the person we supposedly say we love. Premarital sex is a lie — it is full union of the bodies without a total union of the souls. How can we communicate a lie to someone we care about? Marriage is not a permission slip to have sex. Marriage is not a piece of paper, a legal contract, a wedding dress, or a party. Marriage is the union of the two persons — body and soul — with Christ. The activity of sexual intercourse expresses full union whether we want it to or not. Sexual expression in marriage carries with it a ring of truth.

Consider the child. Every child deserves committed parents. Every act of sexual intercourse potentially involves the power of creation. God could have designed us in such a way that sex was a painful endeavor, but in His infinite kindness He made the act of procreation pleasurable for human beings. We, however, have made the pleasure our highest motivation and have tried to invent any technology or chemical that will prevent the procreation! But the truth remains that sex makes babies. There simply is no way to deny it. The modern expression "safe sex" is a lie. There is no birth control short of surgery, natural or artificial, that will eliminate the possibility of having a child. Regardless of how birth control effectiveness is statistically measured, we owe it to our future child to not take the chance that a child may not have committed parents — the principle of justice demands it.

People often say that they are capable of love. Let them prove it. We must love our partner, our self, and our innocent child enough to abstain from sex until marriage. If we are not ready to parent, then we are not ready for marriage. If we are not ready for marriage, then we are not ready for sex. Children deserve the minimum that justice demands; parents who will be there to model committed love that lasts a lifetime. And this is just the beginning, for love demands much more of parents. Children do not require status, fancy clothes, the latest toy, luxurious homes, or college-prep preschools. They need the love of a mom and dad, it's as simple as that. Breeding is easy, father-hood is tough. Sex is fun, motherhood is difficult. To intention-ally create a child outside marital union is to put that child at risk, which is pure selfishness. Even birds provide nests. More and more, we are becoming a nation that is openly hostile to children. We cannot treat children this way. The responsibility is ours. There is no such thing as illegitimate children, only ille-gitimate parents.

Jesus the *Ring-leader* has encircled the act of sexual inter-course in a sacramental union of love. By remaining faithful to our *Lord of the Ring,* we also remain faithful to our Church, our beloved, and our children. As a ring encircles the finger, the com-mitment between a husband and wife will encircle their family in a golden bond of love, and their mutual joy will transform a house into a home.

The ring of truth is a three-note harmony:
   father, mother, and child.
A musical chord that plays God's song.

❧

The normal and real birth control is called self-control.
G.K. Chesterton

Coke

*I will espouse you to me forever. I will espouse you in right
and in justice, in love and in mercy. I will espouse you
in fidelity, and you shall know the Lord.* Hosea 2:21-22

It's funny how advertisements can make an impression on a person, particularly a young person. Having logged enough hours to have acquired the equivalency of a master's degree in TV watching as a child, my mind was filled with assorted audio-visual stimuli. McDonald's songs forever jingled through my brain. Images of Budweiser's Clydesdale horses trotted across my cerebellum. But when it came to slogans, Coke was it. Coke advertisements drenched my memory: *The Pause that Refreshes. Refresh Yourself. A Taste all its Own. Things go better with Coke. Have a Coke and Smile. Can't beat the Feeling. Coke is it. Always Coca-Cola.* But the most impressionable Coke slogan of all that continually fizzled in my cerebral cortex began in 1970:

It's the Real Thing.

"What a great slogan!" I thought as a child. It had worked its magic on me. Though Pepsi and RC Cola might look the same, and basically taste the same, only Coke was the real thing. Or so they had me believing. And believe I did. I wanted no imitations or artificial substitutes. Like Galahad in search of the Holy Grail, like Don Quixote in pursuit of Desdemona, I would settle for nothing less than the *real* thing. Looking back on it, although my gullibility left much to be desired, my quest for truth was admirable. This principle remains a good one, even today, despite my weak childhood application. In all aspects of human relationships, and in particular with love, we should always look for *the real thing*.

Just as real Coke was made from a special secret formula created by Dr. John Pemberton in 1886, real love in romantic relationships follows a special formula created by God. Described in my own words, here is a formula for *love — the real thing:*

> **Love** *is fulfilled only in marriage.*
> **Marriage** *is fulfilled only in life.*
> **Life** *is fulfilled only in God.*

The first statement of the formula might be a bit surprising at first read, but the truth is that real love exists to be completed in marriage. Marriage is the fulfillment of love the same way that baseball is the fulfillment of a ball glove. In marriage, love fits like a glove. This is not only true of romantic love but it is true of all love. A single Christian or a vowed religious person enters into a mystical union or "marriage" with Christ. It is God's will that we all be *married* to Him — meaning each of us must choose to commit ourselves to Christ.

Our mystical *marriage* to Christ can be expressed in several different vocations: husband and wife marriage, the single lifestyle, or religious vows. Each are different expressions of love. The single vocation creates a freedom of possibility. A priest, sister, brother, or single person is not "tied down" to one intimate relationship, which gives them the freedom to share love with many people in rich and diverse ways. Their communal love has a wide focus. They create community rather than procreate a community.

The vocation of marriage creates a freedom of intimacy. A husband and wife are "tied" to each other in an intimate relationship, which limits their freedom to share love with others.

For married couples, their wedding day, a celebration of the birth of an exclusive relationship, is also the death of other potentially intimate relationships. A married man, for example, cannot be too intimate with another woman, for that intimacy belongs with his wife. A couple's capacity for communal service narrows even more with children. The children become their primary obligation. This explains why parents often proclaim, "I used to have a life, now I have children." It is nothing short of incredible the amount of time and energy parenting entails. This is not to say that married people do not have obligations to the human community at large. They do, but first and foremost, they are building community from within. Understanding that romantic love is fulfilled only in marriage, we can now see the problem with the modern notion of "living together" as an alternative to marriage. "Living together" is not real love, because love flows from God and is therefore eternal and enduring. To play it safe by in effect saying "I love you today, but maybe not tomorrow," is not love at all. "Living together" gives couples the pretense of marriage without the self-sacrificing risk that marital love truly entails. It isn't love that lovers desire — it's marriage, just as an arsonist doesn't desire matches, he desires fire. "Living together" is fear's safety net; marriage is a leap of faith. "Living together" is a contract; marriage is a covenant. "Living together" is selfish; marriage is selfless, for the beginning of a marriage is the end of "me." Marriage reveals a love that is willing to risk, to lose, to sacrifice. Such is the real nature of love.

The second statement of the love formula, *marriage is fulfilled only in life*, reveals that the purpose of marriage is not for the man and woman to become each other's life, or to help each other hide from life. Marriage is not life. In marriage, a husband and wife help each other face life and grow spiritually. Marriage helps a couple fulfill their lives. Put simply, a loving relationship is not two people gazing into each other's eyes, but rather both sets of eyes gazing in the same direction. Love relationships are not caves for hiding from life's storms, they are passenger ships navigating us through life's smooth and rough waters. Marriage is not an escape *from* spiritual growth, marriage is designed *for* spiritual growth. A husband and wife are each other's spiritual directors. Love relationships are not designed for indulgence, but for improvement. Love relationships are not about just *finding* the right person, they are about *being* the right person.

The third statement of the love formula, *life is fulfilled only in God*, serves as reminder that for a Christian, life cannot be the final goal of romantic love, because the supreme goal of life is the supreme God. To enter into a Christian marriage is to renounce the "looking glass world" of petty competition, monetary status, rugged individualism, and secular glory and enter a sane wonderland world of sexual intimacy, friendship, and mutual spiritual growth. This has certainly been my experience. Ever since I committed my life to Christ, I have known that I am never alone. But ever since I committed my life to my wife, Colleen, I have never *felt* alone.

It has been said that bad people make bad marriages. This is not exactly true. Bad people who make good choices make good marriages. We are all bad and good to some degree. Marriage is the only place where two wrongs make a right.* The two wrongs are made right by the righteous God. Marriage is not merely a relationship between two persons — that is a contract. Marriage is a covenant — the three become one — man, woman, and God. Contracts are established by men; covenants are established by God.

Our brains will be bombarded with secular and selfish advertisements spun in the name of romantic love. But a true *slo-*

---

* From *Turning Back the Clock*, Peter Kreeft, Ignatius Press, 1994.

gan to recall came from a married woman herself, who at the wedding feast of Cana, instructed servants to:

Do whatever He (Jesus) tells you. (Jn 2:5)

Mary's words apply to the married and non-married alike. Just as Jesus celebrated a marriage by attending a wedding feast in Cana many years ago, He continues to be present in marriages today. Every wedding feast He attends is a prelude to a far greater feast yet to come. So have a Coke and smile. Christ is the love of God incarnate. With Him who is "always love" bonding and leading the sacramental covenant of marriage, we can be certain to have found — *the real thing.*

❧

But lovers do not only desire love; they desire marriage.... (I)f their love for each other is the noblest and freest love conceivable, it can only find its heroic expression in both becoming slaves.

G.K. CHESTERTON

Shield

He went down with them and came to Nazareth, and was obedient to them. His mother meanwhile kept all these things in memory. Jesus, for his part progressed steadily in wisdom and age before God and man.

Luke 2:51-52

As is traditional in many cultures, families have created a shield or crest which symbolically represents their identity, history, and core beliefs. St. Ignatius' shield of the Loyola family displays a wolf, which represents the family's origin in the Basque region of Spain. The English families of Lancaster and York display on their shields a white and red rose respectively. Because of these symbols, their battle for control of the British throne has been named the "War of the Roses." During a legendary ship race to win Irish land, one of the members of the family Ulster cut his hand off and threw it onto the shore, thus ensuring the first claim of ownership for his family. Since then, the Ulster family shield has depicted on it a symbolic red hand. Even John Paul II, the head of the Catholic family has his own blue and gold shield, which includes a large "M" to symbolize his devotion to Mary. But how might the idea of family as a whole be represented on a shield? One suggestion might be a cross surrounded by four symbols: *protection, community, adventure,* and *divinity.*

It is fitting that a shield can be used to represent the family, for parents themselves are *shields* that protect their children from evil. Free to encounter divinity, children can then grow to discover their true humanity. Because of this *protection*, the family is the basic building block of humanity. Our allegiance to family predates our allegiance to nations because, before there were nations, there were families. This is not an accident of nature, it is a divine intention. Family did not begin on earth as a result of random chance; family is a divine creation. God could have created sentient beings that reproduced asexually or homosexually. He chose not to. God willed new life to flow from the committed love of a husband and wife, so that each child could have real love modeled before them.

The strength of the family, therefore, is really an indicator of the strength of the nation. I have often thought that if the United States of America will ever be destroyed, it will not occur from the explosion of a nuclear bomb. America's destruction will result from the implosion of the nuclear family. We will crumble from within, because little by little, the family unit will be subtly and steadily attacked, whether it be from abortion, pornography, casual sex, infanticide, absentee parenting, divorce, neglect, child abuse, etc. If evil can attack the child, it attacks the future. To damage the child is to damage a future parent and family. Harm the family, and there will be a ripple effect of harm throughout the neighborhood, the village, the nation, and eventually the world. That is why the family must be the natural spiritual *shield* that protects a child and raises him to a be a warrior for peace, a seeker of truth, a defender of innocence, an apostle for hope, and a carrier of God's love.

The holy family is the model of a Christian *shield*. They perfected the spirit of the fourth commandment, "Honor thy father and thy mother," by expanding it to include "honor thy child." That is why Christians fight abortion, infanticide, legalized drugs, and casual sex. These forms of child abuse are the evil King Herod's of our day, seeking to kill the Christ-child over and over again. Just as Joseph and Mary shielded the infant Jesus from Herod's evil intent, Christian parents must shield Jesus again, for He dwells in the heart of every child.

I recently ran into a former colleague of mine at church. She was very excited about a new idea she had — starting "basic Christian communities" on the parish level. She was still trying to come up with a name for this new project. I told her that I had been involved in this same enterprise for years. In fact, I already had a name for it. "What do you call this program?" she inquired with much interest. "Family," I replied.

The family is *the* primary Christian *community*, the second symbol on the family shield, which exists in startling contrast to the secular world that surrounds it. It is amazing how our culture deifies the actor, the singer, the general, the athlete, the movie personality, the politician, and the millionaire. These "big stars" are treated as the lights that guide humanity. However, the real "stars" of this world are found in common, everyday people who light the way for others as teachers and healers. And no "star" shines brighter than that of a father and a mother. God did not reveal Himself as our *General*, or as our *President*. He revealed Himself as our *Father* — raising parenthood to the level of the divine. The great Star of the East shown not on Rome or Jerusalem, but on a lowly manger in the tiny village of Bethlehem illuminating the way for "wise men" everywhere to the loving home of the holy family.

> *If we could only bring back into our lives the life that Jesus, Mary, and Joseph lived in Nazareth. If we could make our homes another Nazareth, I think that peace and joy would reign in the world.* Mother Teresa

There are those that say the *family* is an outmoded concept that simply does not fit the modern times. Government, industry, or society must become an alternative to family. We hear politicians cite the expression: "It takes a village to raise a child" as an argument for this new paradigm. But they are wrong. It takes a committed mother and father to raise a child. Speaking as a father, I do not need "the village" to *help* me raise my children, but I do wish it would stop *hurting* me in the raising of my children. The village can assist me by creating a society that is not hostile to children. Yet as Peter Maurin, one of the founders of the Catholic Worker movement, believed, a good society is a society where it is easy to be good. By that standard, our village needs an overhaul. If the family indeed doesn't fit the modern times, then the times ought to be changed to fit the family. As a Christian, I do not wish to be spiritually "ahead of the times." I should rather be two thousand years behind the times, standing alongside the Man from Nazareth. This might seem like backward *thinking* to some, but it is really backward *living* — in the imitation of Christ. Christians have no desire to move *forward* in history, only *upward* beyond history to the Kingdom of God.

I am a theology teacher at a college-prep high school, yet I must confess, my main concern as a parent is not so much what college my daughters may attend, or how much money they may someday earn. These things are only relatively important; they are not essential. I am more concerned about getting my children into a good *heaven* than getting them into a good college. What I desire most, deep down in my heart, is that these beautiful miracles will be with me and my wife forever in the Kingdom of God. I do not want my death to be the end of my relationship with my children. I pray that they will choose Christ and dedicate themselves to being the person that God intended them to be. This is my grown-up Christmas list. This is my wish upon the Morning Star. This is my deepest dream, my most profound hope. As a father, I must dedicate my life to creating a family environment that is conducive for my children to choose Christ. The family is the basic Christian *community*.

Yet around me I still meet fathers who will talk for hours with their child about driving a car, yet remain silent when it comes to sharing their faith. I meet mothers who will make certain their child knows enough mathematics to pass the SAT exam, yet never teach the essentials of the Catholic faith. I meet parents who prefer success and status in their careers to quality and quantity time with their children. They do this despite the fact that I have never heard of a father on his deathbed, saying, "I wish I would have spent more time at the office." Instead we pay others to carry out our vocational responsibilities. We claim that we don't have the time to parent when the truth is that we lack the passion or the will to do that difficult job ourselves. I don't know of anyone for hire who can love a child as much as their father and mother. So children continue to cry for love and instead receive new toys. They long to be held but instead get designer clothes. They imitate television instead of imitating Dad. Children are best *home*made, not store-bought. Familial love is priceless, something money cannot buy. Creating a happy home should be our highest ambition.

There is an unpredictability to family, and this wildness provides an opportunity for heroism. Our third symbol on the family *shield* would depict this, for the family is an *adventure* and not a computer program. As children, we didn't pick the family we are born into, nor as parents can we control the personalities of the children we bring into our family. Young couples who say, "We want to wait until we are ready to have children," may not have realized that parents are *never* fully ready for children! For example, I would never have predicted that, as a father of all girls, my head would be filled with the names of the entire Von Trapp family from *The Sound of Music*, or the names of all the American Girl Collection dolls (Felicity, Kirsten, Addie, etc.). But such are the interests of my daughters. I had assumed I would be playing Batman and football with sons, but instead I know all about the *Little House on the Prairie* and the Boxcar children! Like all great adventures, family provides an opportunity for challenge and growth.

And this is no *mild* adventure. It is a voyage of epic proportion. Fatherhood is tough. Motherhood is laborious work. Many a day ends with a parent falling hard on his or her bed, exhausted or exasperated. It is certainly the hardest thing I have ever done or ever will do. Before my first child was born, I asked a friend what being a parent was like. He replied, "It's chipping. Chipping away slowly every ounce of selfishness that you have in you." He was right. As with a hero in any *adventure* story, it is our task to transform random uncontrollableness into the opportunity for love. For love is the measure of any happy ending, and the collective result of our applied love will shape our children's souls, and make heaven a reality on earth.

Finally, our family *shield* would not be complete without a fourth symbol representing *divinity*. For the family is even more than an intention of the divine, it is also the very nature of God Himself. God exists in His nature as three Persons in one Being. The Father loves the Son. The Son loves the Father. And the love between them is so perfect, that the love is a Person, the Spirit. Like a reflector pointing heavenward, we *mirror* the nature of God in the family. The husband loves his wife. The wife loves her husband. And that love is so blessed, that the love itself becomes a person, the child. That is why the best way for a husband to love his children is to love his wife, and vice versa. The family is a living witness to the nature of God himself.

Protection, community, adventure, and *divinity* — these make up the *shield* that is the family. Family is an endeavor of unparalleled importance. It can and should be overwhelming. This is no mere human task. Though children don't come to us complete with a *manual*, there is no need for worry or fear. In faith, we can take comfort from the fact that each child comes complete with an *Emmanuel*.

Let the divine adventure begin in each of our families. This is my wish for all mom's and dad's, that together with our children may we roll in autumn leaves, dance through daring stories, laugh through timeworn jokes, kneel together in prayer, watch long summer sunsets, and feast often at the family table. May we together sing lullabies at bedtime, make hot embers glow in the fireplace, and build friendly snowmen. May we daily plant on our children the words "I love you" and marvel at their beauty, as we do the spring flowers. May we comfort them in their tears, celebrate their triumphs, cherish their innocence, guard fiercely their purity, praise their goodness, and punish their wrong doings. May we love each other's weaknesses, develop each other's strengths, and never stop hugging our children — no matter how old we, or they, may be. May we cement love's foundation and send their hearts Godward, toward the eternal festival of family.

Disorder in the society is a result of disorder in the family.

St. Angela Merici

Horton the Elephant

> *Whoever receives one child such as this in my name receives me; and whoever receives me, receives not me but the One who sent me.*   Mark 9:37

It is said that an elephant never forgets. Horton the Elephant can teach us what ought to be an unforgettable truth. In Dr. Seuss' wonderful book, *Horton Hears A Who*, an elephant, the largest of animals, reveals the intrinsic worth of even the smallest of humans. Horton discovers an entire world of people living on a dust speck. All of the other animals, not aware of this tiny humanity, see Horton as crazy and try to destroy what Horton holds so dear. Despite great risk to himself, Horton defends the small and innocent. In writing this book, Dr. Seuss wrote a beautiful story that can apply to the unborn child, for art can take on a life apart from the artist.

> *"I'll just have to save him. Because after all…*
> *A person's a person, no matter how small."*

Let's face it, if we really want to break up a party, we can always bring up the topic of abortion. Discussing the humanity of an unborn child makes politicians stammer and media stars wince. I know of no more controversial an issue. It divides brother against brother, child against parent, bringing uncivil *war* into the family and the nation. The problem's legal roots can be traced back to 1857, when nine of the supposedly most intelligent men in the land ruled that blacks were not persons according to the

U.S. Constitution (*Dred Scott* decision). Blacks could be bought, sold, or killed at the discretion of the owner. The Southern slave states wanted the Northern abolitionists to respect their legal "right to choose" to enslave their fellow human beings. Finally, a civil war later, we amended the Constitution to stop discrimination on the basis of color. I strongly suspect that 170 years ago, people knew that blacks were persons, but cultural convenience and financial desires overrode their capacity to stop the evil. Minds were used, not to seek the truth, but to rationalize that tragic institution. Now, let us compare this historical situation to the abortion debate.

> *Some sort of creature of very small size.*
> *Too small to be seen by an elephant's eyes.*

In 1973, nine of the supposedly most intelligent men in the land ruled that an unborn child is not a person according to the U.S. Constitution (*Roe v. Wade*). Unborn children could be bought, sold, or killed at the discretion of the owner, which was ruled to be the mother. Many people wanted the pro-life citizens, modern-day abolitionists, to respect their legal "right to choose" to destroy their fellow human beings. Despite the *civil war* of words and political action, the Constitution remains unchanged, and we have yet to stop this discrimination on the basis of age. I strongly suspect that people today know, deep down, that a pregnant woman has a baby inside her, but cultural convenience and financial desires continue to override our capacity to stop the evil. Minds are used, not to seek the truth, but to rationalize this tragic institution.

> *The Wickersham Brothers came shouting, "What rot!*
> *This elephant's talking to Who's who are not!"*

The issue comes down to a decision as to whether or not the fetus is *property*, simply a part of the woman's body, or a *person* endowed with basic human rights. If the fetus is property, then no one should ever be "personally opposed" to an abortion any more than they should be personally opposed to an appendectomy. Surgery designed to remove an organ should cause no moral outcry. If the fetus is property, let's have as many abortions as we fancy. However, if the fetus *is* a unique genetic human life, distinct from the mother, then the law should protect the unborn child's fundamental right to live. The government's primary task is the safeguarding of human rights. It exists primarily for this purpose. No one has the ambiguous "right to choose" any more than they have the right to choose to rape or mutilate. If we allow even one innocent child to die, such as in the case of rape, then we have opened a Pandora's box for justifying the legal death of other innocent lives. Our rights end where another person's rights begin. Is the fetus a unique human life? The scientific answer is, undeniably, yes! He or she is *human*, with a new set of 23 pairs of chromosomes with a unique DNA coding in each cell beginning at conception; and he or she is *alive*, demonstrating all the characteristics of biological life — growth, response to stimulus, nutritional process, respiration, etc. Therefore, the unborn child is a *human life*. He or she is not a "potential human being," but rather an "actual human being" with potential.

Our Christian faith gives us insights into the human condition. Martin Luther King, Jr., for example, used Christian theology to articulate his opposition to segregation, even though segregation was a human rights issue that was not limited to Christians alone. Dorothy Day used her Christian conversion to inspire her work with the poor, despite the fact that homelessness was a human rights issue that concerns all Americans. Christians today use their "sanctity of life" ethic to oppose legal abortion, even though abortion is a human rights issue which transcends any particular religious dogma. Moral issues apply to everyone. Atheists can acknowledge a child's humanity and act to defend the child, and many have. Many defending life are not crusading under the name of Christ, yet Christ, nonetheless, is crusading in them.

[He] begged, "please don't harm all my little folks, who
Have as much right to live as us bigger folks do!"

We also must be wary of Christians themselves who might be attacking the child in the name of Christ. Some contemporary moral theologians, for example, have argued that, since the fetus is not viable, it is not a person to be defended. This argument, based on dependency, is the complete antithesis of the teachings of Christ. Our humanity is not defined by whether or not we are dependent, by what we can or cannot do, but by who we are. Personhood isn't lost by being dependent; we are all dependent. Personhood isn't lost by being handicapped; we are all handicapped. It's just that some handicaps are more visible than others. Down-syndrome children and other severely handicapped individuals have much to teach us if we listen. Christianity has always taught that if a person is weak, they deserve *more* help, not less. Whatsoever we do to the *least* of our brothers and sisters, we do unto Christ Himself. That is why we fight the slaughter of innocents, and the sexism and casual sex that place women in fearful circumstances. But we never should fight evil with evil. Violence in word or deed can never promote life. Let our only armaments be love and truth, to defend Christ in a distressing disguise.

We've GOT to make noises in greater amounts!
So open your mouth, lad! For every voice counts!

Jesus, divinity wrapped in swaddling humanity, came to us as a holy embryo, and then a fetus. Though Mary's circumstances would make her the ideal candidate for abortion by today's standards — young, unmarried, and at risk — Mary saw herself not as "queen of her child" but rather "maidservant of the Lord." Thank God. Thank Mary. And Joseph became the model for all adoptive parents. Jesus was not a child of his flesh but a child of his love. Thank Joseph. So despite King Herod's wrath, the precious Christ child was born so that we might be born-again.

They've proved they ARE persons, no matter how small.
And their whole world was saved by the Smallest of All!

There are Herods still among us, whether motivated by fear, ignorance, selfishness or profit. They kill behind clean, sterilized walls where no one can see or hear the pain. But Christian "wise men" will oppose Herod and follow the stars of love and life that guide our children home. There will always be room in our inn for the unborn child. Be like an elephant. Don't forget. Don't forget the children. They are the innocent and voiceless. But if we hear with our hearts, we can hear their cries, and wrap them in swaddling love.

❧

The Eternal Being, who knows everything and
who created the whole universe, became not only a
man, but before that a baby, and before that
a fetus inside a woman's body.

C.S. LEWIS

Gravity

*If you live according to my teaching, you are truly my
disciples: then you will know the truth, and the truth will
set you free.*   John 8:32

There is an invisible force in the world that is binding on all of
us. We call it gravity. It compresses and connects us to the surface of the planet. It is so omnipresent that we barely notice it
most of the time. But notice it or not, it still affects us. Astronauts orbiting the earth are able to float in space because, being
farther away from the planet surface, they experience a weaker
gravitational pull. In fact, because of the weaker amount of force
exerted on astronauts in a space station, they discovered that their
bodies had actually grown two inches in length. Amazing. As a
child, I thought that gravity was an "up-down" phenomenon, as
simple as Newton's apple falling to the ground. As an adult, my
own strange description of *gravitational law* is: a scientific term
used to describe the phenomenon that "things stick together and
we don't know why." We stick "down" to the earth's surface simply because it is the largest "thing" near us. Gravity describes
"how" we stick together; however, it cannot answer "why" we
stick together.

There is another invisible force in the world that is binding on all of us. We call it morality. It compels and connects us
to our fellow members of the planet. It is so omnipresent that
we barely notice it most of the time. But notice it or not, it still
affects us. Amoral persons are able to float through life because,
being further away from their common humanity, they experi-

ence a weaker moral "pull." In fact, because of the weaker amount of force exerted on their souls, an individual's conscience can actually decay. Appalling. As a child, I thought that morality was a "black-white" phenomenon, as simple as obeying only the exact proscription of Moses' Ten Commandments. As an adult, my own strange description of *moral law* is: a religious term used to describe the phenomenon that "people should stick together and we do know why." Morality describes "how" we should treat ourselves and one another, and faith can answer "why" we stick together.

One of the great intellectual errors of the 20th century lies in morality and religion being relegated to the category of *subjective opinion*. This is a critical flaw. Just as there is a *gravitational law* that is binding on our bodies, there is a *moral law* that is binding on our souls.

"What right do you have to impose your morality on me?" I was once asked by a pro-choice advocate. "I am human," I replied. "Human beings are obligated to do what is right. If we don't, the innocent get hurt. It isn't *my* morality, anyway. Humanity didn't invent moral law, we discovered it. Besides, you seem quite content to allow a mother to impose her pro-abortion opinion on her unborn child."

Needless to say, I was unsuccessful in changing her mind. People tend to change only when they want to change. She was like an aircraft carrier who refused to alter course. Consider this actual emergency ban radio conversation*:

#1 *Please divert your course 15 degrees to the North to avoid a collision.*

#2 *Recommend you divert YOUR course 15 degrees to South to avoid a collision.*

---

* Taken from the Internet Site "Caser's Celtic Pages — Jokes 'R Us"

#1 *This is the Captain of a U.S. Navy ship. I say again, divert YOUR course.*

#2 *No. I say again, you divert YOUR course.*

#1 *THIS IS THE AIRCRAFT CARRIER ENTERPRISE, WE ARE A LARGE WARSHIP OF THE U.S. NAVY. DIVERT YOUR COURSE NOW!*

#2 *This is a lighthouse. Your call.*

The moral lighthouse cannot change. We can either see the light and alter our course accordingly, or ignore it at our own risk. Moral law is as constant as gravitational law, in fact, even more constant. Our call.

If we take moral law out of the category of *objective truth*, then in our moral thinking, personal opinion becomes absolute. The effect of this philosophical disaster will be threefold. First, *we will lose the authority to impose morality* on another person. This is implied in the statement "I'm entitled to my opinion." Though we may have the legal right to speak, that doesn't make what we say true. As the Catholic apologist Peter Kreeft wrote: "A person has no more right to a false opinion than a stomach has a right to poison." To disagree with this view is to imply that it is false, which proves the point.

A second debacle resulting from consigning moral truth to opinion, is that *popular opinion will become a substitute for morality*. Under the guise of mob rule, political correctness, or legal law, popular opinion will become the highest statement of what is right. Law becomes morality, instead of law flowing from morality. Arthur, the legendary once and future king of the British Isles, fought this mentality. As he discovers in the play *Camelot*, justice is found not in "might *makes* right," but in "might *for* right." If we abandon this majestic insight, law, born for the purpose of ensuring human rights will be reborn for the purpose of protecting human wrongs.

A third philosophical repercussion resulting from making

personal opinion absolute, will be that *feelings will drive our decisions rather than moral principles*. If this occurs, our unethical ethic will be based on "feeling good" rather than on "being good." Without reason guiding emotion, we will move through our life like a ship without a rudder. Pleasure will replace love as the greatest good. And selfishness, the mortal enemy of morality, will triumph. The loss of personal morality will be commensurate with a loss of personal integrity.

These changes can have devastating consequences to human history, but maybe most profoundly, they can alter our understanding of the nature of religion. Disassociate religion from justice and justice becomes lame and unfounded. Disassociate justice from religion and religion becomes blind and dangerous. There is a necessary link between morality and religion. If moral law is a human idea, instinct, or contract, then it would have no real authority over us, because we would be free to ignore it if we wish. But moral law is not a human invention. Therefore, the only reasonable conclusion would be that it comes from God. Only *The Ultimate* would have ultimate authority. Thomas Jefferson understood this theo-logical connection when he proclaimed in the *Declaration of Independence* that inalienable human rights are endowed upon us by our Creator. Rules point to a Ruler. Laws point to a Lawmaker. Fyodor Dostoevsky reaffirmed this when he warned us in *The Brothers Karamazov*, "If there is no God, then everything is permissible." Remove God from morality, and in time, morality will be removed from humanity. And if this occurs, God help us all.

In practical politics, it may be necessary to allow some separation between religious dogma and morality in state affairs, but there never should be an absolute separation between them. Nor can there ever be. That would make atheism the state religion and humanity the highest authority. And absolute power corrupts absolutely. Anything that becomes a god becomes a demon.

In practical life, morality has to guide our entire life. We cannot create a false dichotomy between our private life and our public life. We have but one life to live. Morality is a coat woven and worn as a seamless garment. Though in politics church and state may require some separation, church and state cannot be separate in us. If we separate ourselves from morality, we separate ourselves from our common humanity. Moral law based on *objective truth* is our lighthouse from beyond. When wrestling with moral issues, we are playing "high stakes" poker. If murder is wrong, it is wrong for everyone. If premarital sex is wrong, it is wrong for everyone. If abusing drugs is wrong, it is wrong for everyone. Our moral actions cannot be a "candle in the wind," bent and blown out by changing times. Moral actions are an "eternal flame," unyielding and timeless, enlightening the human community with justice and goodness. We cannot allow moral laws, and therefore human rights, to be violated. As Edmund Burke warned us:

> *The only thing necessary for the triumph of evil is for good men (and women) to do nothing.*

Humans are not gods. We try to obey a moral law that is greater than ourselves. C.S. Lewis believed that two facts were the foundation of *all* clear thinking about ourselves and the universe we live in. Fact 1, *there is a moral law.* Fact 2, *we break it.* Lewis adds a second important fact here. Moral law flows from *The Perfect One,* but we will not be able to follow it perfectly. Absolute principles guide very "un-absolute" men. We must not let our inability lower the absolute standard, in thought or action. Mercy and forgiveness toward men, but never compromise the truth. Ideas are more powerful than bullets. Behind moral decay is first the decay of moral thinking. No person, no family, no community, no country can flourish unless it is grounded in morality. We must try to abide by objective moral law just as we must abide by objective gravitational law. To ignore either is its own punishment. We need to appreciate the *gravity* of the situation.

❧

The time is always right to do what is right.
MARTIN LUTHER KING, JR.

Black

Your love must be sincere. Detest what is evil, cling to what is good.   Romans 12:9

Once upon a time, in a galaxy close, close by, an evil Imperial Empire attempted to dominate the universe. But guided by the unseen power of "the force," a young-at-heart band of rebels fought against the forces of darkness to keep the galaxy free. These are words that could have come from the science fiction trilogy *Star Wars*, but they also describe the reality of *Spiritual Wars*: the cosmic battle between good and evil.

Consider two questions that relate to one another. The first is about natural color; the second refers to God. The first question is, *Is black a color?* The answer is "no," black is not a color. It is the absence of color. It's real; it is just not a color. White is the source of all color, and it always comes from some*thing* — a star. White light shining through a prism will reveal a spectrum containing all colors. Darkness doesn't "begin" from anywhere; it is the absence of light. The second related question is, *Since God created everything, did God create evil?* The answer is "no," evil is not a thing. It is the abuse of good. It's real; it is just not a thing. God is the source of all goodness; all things come from a Some*one* — God. God shining through His creation will reveal a multitude of goodness. The darkness of evil doesn't "begin" anywhere; it is the absence of good. We can think of black, then, as an *anti-color*. We can think of the presence of evil, then, as that which is *anti-Christ*.

No wonder the popular film *Star Wars* used "black and white" imagery to be a representation of the spiritual battle. Three characters in particular illustrate three aspects of good and evil. The "master of evil," Darth Vader, is dressed completely in *black* and is controlled by the *dark side* of the force. Luke Skywalker, the hero apprenticed to become a Jedi knight for justice, is dressed in white and is learning the ways of "the force." Han Solo, initially depicted as a lone wolf out only for himself, is dressed in both black and white, an undecided rebel without a noble cause. He, like us, must choose between the forces of good and the forces of evil.

But many of us remain "in the dark" regarding the nature of evil. This confusion dates far into the past to the origins of humanity. In "the Fall" we chose to allow evil into our souls and into our world. Once this Pandora's box was opened, evil became shadowy and misunderstood in the minds and hearts of mankind. The clarity that humility had given us was replaced by the illusion of pride. Instead of seeing evil as evil, sin distorted our spiritual vision. Therefore, the most fundamental truth to regain regarding the nature of evil is that *evil appears good.*

A few years ago, there was a television magazine show that featured an exorcism in its first half-hour. For weeks after, all my students wanted to do was discuss this. But I told them that there was more satanic activity in the *second* half-hour than in the first. This puzzled them for awhile, until they recalled that the second half featured a story about the "wild" happenings going on in Florida during Spring Break by college kids. That was more dangerous because the college antics didn't automatically *appear* evil. My point was to try to create an awareness not only of extraordinary supernatural evil, but also an awareness of evil dressed up in the ordinary natural form of "fun." Few doubt that a Hollywood movie such as *The Exorcist* is dealing with the theme of evil. But they don't easily recognize the promotion of evil in a movie such as *Animal House.* Evil appears good, that's why we choose it. Its nature is to deceive. Premarital sex and getting drunk look good, that's why we are drawn to them. Sinning looks fun, that's why we sin. Evil is like a liar. A liar would never declare "I am a liar." That would be telling the truth. A liar would always proclaim the opposite and say, "I am a truthteller." This is mankind's dilemma with evil. Paul understood this when he wrote "Satan disguises himself as an angel of light" (2 Cor 11:14).

A second critical truth that casts some light on the nature of evil is that *evil is habitual.* Like a ship caught in a whirlpool, the more we act on an evil thought or deed, the stronger the force of the habit becomes. Like centripetal force, it drives us downward toward its center, causing us to lose more and more free will as the force builds. That is why we can never choose an evil, even the lesser of two evils, as a legitimate alternative to good. Choose evil and its force within us becomes stronger. Supporting the enemy is no way to win spiritual warfare. Some might justify giving in to the "dark side" by speciously arguing that we can only know an evil by actually doing it. We can't judge marijuana until we have at least smoked it, they argue. But a judge does not have to have murdered someone in order to judge a murder case. In fact, a juror who had murdered would automatically be considered prejudicial and be removed from the jury. Participating in an evil only clouds our judgment. The truth is that we can only know the real nature of a temptation by *resisting* it. It is only by standing against the current in a stream that a person can know the true force of the water. This is why Jesus had such incredible insight into human temptation and evil. By perfectly resisting evil, Jesus had a perfect understanding of its real nature. Even the *Jedi Master* Yoda from *Star Wars* understood the habitual nature of evil:

> *Once you start down the dark path, forever will it dominate your destiny.*

Even legally mitigating evil increases the power and effect of evil in a society. Legalize drugs and there will be more availability, temptation, addiction, and violence. Educate young people to use condoms and there will be more unwanted pregnancies due to more teens experiencing sexual intercourse. Legalize prostitution and more people will experiment with it due to its accessibility and its pretense of legitimacy. Legally, as well as personally, choosing evil always makes it stronger, which makes us weaker. A choice made between two evils ignores the third possibility of choosing a good. If we give up on striving for goodness, either personally or socially, the habitual force of evil will give evil a power it should not have to destroy humanity. Again, as Master Yoda said to young Luke:

> Once you start down the dark path, forever will it dominate your destiny.

Despite its parasitic power, *evil is not an equal force with good* in the universe. God could destroy all evil by batting a single eyelash. But He won't. To destroy evil is to destroy free will, and the possibility for love. God allows evil, He does not will it. And there is no evil that is so horrendous that God cannot bring good from it. Evil is a temporary disease that infects the human soul, which Christ has already cured. He can vaccinate us with His very being. Just as a single candle can pierce through an entire room of darkness, the light of Christ has pierced the darkness of sin and evil. Good can and will triumph over evil.

So where might a young Jedi knight begin the battle against evil? In government? In the media? In schools? In the church? No, we must begin at the beginning, by allowing Christ to work at evil's origin — in our *thoughts*. Wars must be fought in our souls before they can be fought among the stars. Before every action there is first a thought which is shaped by the ideas and images we receive. The marketplace of ideas and the world of images have a powerful effect on our minds. The heart and mind is the primeval battlefield, where angels and demons, saints and sinners, clash for supremacy. The film *The Empire Strikes Back*, illustrates this insight. In one scene, the wise Yoda bids Luke Skywalker to enter into a mystical cave. In the cave, Luke confronts an illusory Darth Vader and cuts off his head. But when Luke peers into Vader's dark mask, it explodes and reveals Luke's own face. The symbolism is clear. Luke's first enemy to conquer and control is himself. He must do battle with the darkness, the evil within. Only after this is understood, can he be "the return of a *Jedi*." A son must save himself before he can save his father. What is true for Luke is true for all of us. We must choose to be an instrument for good rather than evil, and then bring this conviction to our world. We propose goodness as the solution, mindful that we are also part of the problem. The ultimate solution is Jesus. He who is light without darkness, love without sin, good without evil, will battle where angels fear to tread. We need only to be on His winning team. With Christ as our *Jedi Master*, we can be a rebel *force* for the Kingdom of God. When faced with the darkness of evil, the light of God's empire will strike back.

❧

*Occupy your minds with good thoughts, or the
enemy will fill them with bad ones.
Unoccupied, they cannot be.*

THOMAS MORE

Toys

My son, use freely whatever you have and enjoy it as best you can.   Sirach 14:11

"Play with your own toys!" I yelled. This was directed at my two year-old daughter Clare. Neither of us was having a fun day. A handful of assorted ragamuffins had been invited over to our house for playgroup, and they were attacking Clare's pile of toys with exuberance. They were having a great time. Clare was not. She was less than thrilled with the mandatory "sharing of toys" that had been forced upon her. No matter what toy she had, she wanted to play with one that another toddler had. When she finally got the toy she coveted, she would immediately lose interest in it and seek a toy being played with by another child. She was the living embodiment of greed, an "Ebenezer Clare," as any two-year-old can be. Anyone raising children has empirical proof of original sin. Again and again, I had to tell Clare to be satisfied with the toys that she had. Finally, after I said these words for the 200th time, a thought came to me. Maybe that's what God has been saying to me all these years. We grown-ups act a lot like two-year-olds. Perhaps God has been telling each of us, over and over again: *"Play with your own toys!"*

There are two ways to consider my toy revelation. First, if we allow *toys* to refer to God-given traits and abilities, then *"Play with your own toys!"* means *"Be happy with who you are."* How much of our lives are spent wanting someone else's looks, someone else's size, someone else's abilities? We expend enormous amounts of energy wanting to be someone other than who we are, like a two-year-old wanting only the toy she doesn't have. What a tragic waste! We need to take inventory of our unique qualities, then direct them *ad majorem Dei gloriam,* to the greater glory of God. There is a reason why God made us the way He did. He had a purpose beyond our understanding. We can trust Him. He knows what He's doing. Instead of crying like a two-year-old because we lack a certain charm, we ought to appreciate who we are and what we have. If God values us as we are, who are we to disagree with Him? Jesus' commandment to love our neighbor as ourselves presupposes a love of self. If we do not love ourselves we are incapable of loving another, for we can't give what we don't have. God's message to His childish sons and daughters is the message that I gave to my daughter Clare: We should be playing with our own toys. To do this, we must first appreciate our gifts, then develop them, and finally let the playing begin. Our acceptance of who we are can foster a *childlike* instead of *childish* attitude in us, and we can be like babes in toyland.

The second way to consider my toy revelation is to have the word *toys* refer to personal possessions and property. Then *"Play with your own toys!"* means, *"Be happy with what you have."* Spiritual poverty is always wanting more. Greed compels us to forever thirst for water even when we're not thirsty. My daughter Clare and her fellow toddlers are not the only ones who suffer from this affliction. The difference between men and boys is the price of their toys. The challenge is the same, only the toys have changed. Do I possess my possessions or do my possessions possess me? Do I own things or do they own me? Do I value life to enjoy all things, or do I value things so as to enjoy life? Possessions can be like magnets that cling to our sin-steeled hearts, weighing us down with a burden we need not bear. In such a wealthy country as the United States, it is easy to *acquire* rather than *aspire.* The acquisition of material wealth can take on "religious" proportions. We can become a culture desperate to seek the perfect some*thing* instead of the perfect Some*one*. In his book *Denial of Death*, psychologist Ernest Becker offered this indictment of our materialist culture:

> *Modern man is drinking and drugging himself out of awareness, or he spends his time shopping, which is the same thing.*

In Luke's Gospel, Jesus challenges a rich man to come follow Him, but first the man must sell all he has and give the money to the poor. This was not a metaphor. It was a direct challenge. Jesus looked right through the rich man's eyes and into his heart, and cut through all the defense mechanisms he had created to shelter his greed. The rich man did not understand how poor his money had truly made him. Christ offered him "the needle's eye" as an antidote to his greed. It was a bitter medicine to heal his sick heart.

How might this "riches to rags" story apply to us? Must each of us give *all* our possessions away? Perhaps. St. Francis of Assisi did. But for most of us, perhaps not. Not all are called to the radical poverty that Francis lived out. Maybe the story of the rich man can apply to us in answering a different question. What is "the needle's eye" that Christ is asking us to pass through? The answer lies in any treasure that we have placed ahead of our God. Christ, as always, offers us healing. Though each person is unique, "a needle's eye" awaits us all.

> *If you cannot take out a hammer and shatter into a hundred pieces a rock CD that promotes the dehumanization of women, then you are enslaved to musical pleasure. Are you the "rich man" to whom Jesus is speaking?*
>
> *If your chosen lifestyle forces you to put career status and*

the acquisition of material things over your children, family, or friends, are you the "rich man" to whom Jesus is speaking?

If you look down on others who do not possess your style of quality clothes, vacations, car, house, etc., are you the "rich man" to whom Jesus is speaking?

We are all the "rich man." *All* of our possessions must be given back to the One who gave them to us in the first place. And any that are returned are done so only to be used for His greater glory. We must give up everything — our dreams, hopes, desires, toys, etc. — and subordinate them to God's design. He knows the master plan for us because He is the Master. God knows what is best for us, for He is the author of our destiny. Andrew abandoned his nets and followed Jesus. Matthew put away his tax tables and followed Jesus. We, like them, have to face all the glamour the world has to offer and choose Jesus instead.

When we measure the cost of this surrender, it is a paltry sum, considering what we will receive in return. There is a healing power to any earthly loss, a heavenly simplicity and freedom to be found. If a vessel is filled to the brim with water, it can hold no wine. To possess the wine, the water must first be emptied from the vessel. To possess Christ, we must empty ourselves first. His eternal wine tastes infinitely better than our water. A fist clenched tightly to hold on to *something* is not open to receive the once-broken, nail-torn hand of the *Someone* who loves us. A heart filled with "what the world holds sacred" can never receive the Sacred Heart. Make room for *Abba*.

Imagine that through a smoke-filled room, with fire raging all around us, we see a small baby crying and a priceless Van Gogh painting. Assume we can only bring one of these two to safety. Which would we choose? Christians always choose the person — personalism over materialism, goodness over material goods. We follow the Golden Rule, not the rule of gold. C.S. Lewis was once asked "What books would be with us in heaven?" He replied, "Only the ones we gave away on earth." His answer is clear even to a two-year-old — persons over possessions, life over lifestyles, joys over toys. To truly enjoy *toys*, whether it refers to who we are or what we have, *toys* must be subordinate to the Source of all joy — God. The ultimate Toymaker is also the ultimate Joymaker.

> *Let Jesus be our only prized possession and we will be possessed by Him who prized us.*

All you have shall some day be given; therefore give now, that the season of giving may be yours and not your inheritors.

KAHLIL GIBRAN

The Monster

In the last days men will be lovers of self... lovers of pleasure rather than lovers of God.   2 Timothy 3:1, 4

A remote dark castle looms on the horizon. Lightning strikes the forbidden citadel and the electrical power finds its way to the dungeon laboratory of an evil scientist. "It's alive!" he screams, as a piecemeal corpse becomes animated into... the monster Frankenstein!

The silver screen has immortalized this famous image of horror and fear. But the original book points to a different monster. Mary Wollstencraft Shelley penned the post-Renaissance classic *Frankenstein* when she was only 19 years old. In the original story published in 1818, the real monster is not the creature but the "creator" of the creature. Dr. Victor Frankenstein is far more monstrous than the hideous beast he creates. The grotesque "experiment" is more a victim of Dr. Frankenstein's hubris. It is the evil doctor who plays "god" without regard to moral consequence. He rejects the natural law that guides both sexuality and science, and he refuses to take responsibility for his own recklessness. But it is he who dies in the end — a fate fitting for those who wish to kill Truth. The monstrous creature, on the other hand, simply vanishes at the end of the story.

Shelley's tale of fright flew right in the face of a prevailing mentality begun within the Enlightenment, which held that humanity should no longer be shackled under oppressive moral and religious restraints. Reason, the enlightenment believed, divorced from faith would "enlighten" mankind. Shelley rejected this thesis. She believed that if we ignore or reject human nature, nature will return dressed up as *horror*. The creative urge, unbound by moral and spiritual consideration, becomes monstrous. The dream of usurping the power of God can only end in nightmare. Shelley even subtitled the book "The Modern Prometheus," which is an allusion to a mythological figure that stole fire from the gods. If we divorce sexuality and science from the wisdom of God, then the triumph of a modern Prometheus will bring nothing but tragedy.

I have chilling news to bring. The danger signaled by Shelley in her fictional 19th century book has come to pass in the factual 20th century. The monster has reappeared and is among us. Dr. Frankenstein has become an *artist*, and his *art*, removed from the confines of morality and religion, has become a hideous creature. *Art*, once for God's sake, has become "art for art's sake." Unshackled from moral restraints, art is now free to become a monster that will enslave. Just as science unchained can chain humanity, so too, can art. This en*light*enment mentality can only *blind* humanity. Hundreds of years before Shelley, the Greek philosopher Plato warned us of this same danger:

> *Through foolishness they deceived themselves into think-ing that there was no right or wrong in music — that it was to be judged good or bad solely by the pleasure that it gave.*

When my students speak about a "good movie" or a "good song," they rarely are referring to *goodness*. Yet goodness is an attribute of God. In order to reconnect the words *good* and *God* in their minds, I have asked them in the past to give examples of "good movies" and "good songs." After they cite some examples, I ask them to insert the word *God* into the phrases instead of *good* and see if they would still consider them "God movies" or "God songs." They often realize that their usage of the word *good* is quite different from their understanding of *God*.

This removal of religion and morality from artistic criticism is not unique to my students. Their thinking is a reflection of how the mass media approaches art. The majority of music and movie critics are more interested in artistic form than spiritual substance. In hundreds of art reviews I have read, rarely does the writer consider the moral content of a story or song. They give entertainment and artistic evaluations, seldom moral insights. At the turn of the century, G.K. Chesterton, the Catholic journalist, identified the beginnings of this trend in his fellow British writers. He predicted a monstrous trend that has since come true:

> *If the modern world will not insist on having some sharp and definite moral law, capable of resisting the counter-attraction of art and humor, the modern world will simply be given over as a spoil to anybody who manages to do a nasty thing in a "nice" way* (quotation marks added).

As usual, G.K.C. was right on target. An evil can be promoted if it is enticing and deceiving, and it can be done under the guise that "art cannot be morally judged." But if art is not under the dominion of God, then it becomes its own "god" — a "monster" that does good or evil at its own whim. That is why the Christian approach to art makes the moral evaluation the highest priority. In order to "understand" art, art needs to "stand under" God.

Our evaluation should be threefold. First, we can respond to the *entertainment value* of art, asking the question, "Is this emotionally pleasing to *me?*" Second, we can examine the *artistic value* of art, asking the question, "Is this intellectually pleasing to *me?*" Finally, and most importantly, we should evaluate the *moral value* of art, asking the question, "Is this pleasing to *God?*" Since Christianity values God over self, the answer to this question is of ultimate importance. Christ is the *King of Hearts* that trumps the *Queen of Arts* or the *Jesting Joker* in the card game of artistic criticism. Saying it even simpler, if Jesus is *for* the art, we can be for it. If Jesus is *against* it, we should be against it. Popular art as well as fine art needs to be judged by the simple standard of Jesus. We cannot place emotional or artistic *pleasure* over our commitment to Christ. It's that simple.

What is not always simple is making the determination of whether or not we can support any particular television show or rock song. The judgment is not always crystal clear. But at least making the attempt to consider Jesus indicates a serious-ness of faith. That alone would be a significant step in restrain-ing the unbound art world. Besides, in many cases, art that pro-motes the demeaning of language, children, family, women, sexuality, organized religion, God, etc. shows clear signs of be-ing the artistic monster. That is why we need the guidance of Scripture and Church tradition. We cannot let any confusion cloud our recognition of moral danger. If Jesus is attacked in name, in symbol, or in the human family, we must fight the monster, for whoever profits from an evil sustains it. We should defend our best Friend, for He defended us when we most needed it.

Paradoxically, when we defend Christ we are really defend-ing ourselves. Everything we see or hear has a spiritual effect on us, whether we are aware of it or not. Ignoring poison while we drink it does not negate the fact that it is poison. Art can inspire or demean. We cannot underestimate the power of art to shape our perceptions and choices. Although art is not *directly* respon-sible for any human choice, it is *indirectly* responsible in that it can act as a catalyst for good or evil, just as a drug pusher is indi-rectly responsible for drug abuse, encouraging the evil of addic-tion. The Dr. Frankensteins of the art world, and the public who support their creations, need to be held morally accountable. Failure to do so would be at our own expense. Monsters tend to devour the innocent first.

We should expect a battle. The two lightning rods in these culture wars are the entertainment industry and the Roman Catholic Church. They are the largest institutions that can wage spiritual war over the role of art in a society. A moral and religious evaluation can come down to choosing either Holly*wood* or the *wood* of the cross. It is not surprising that many modern movie and television scripts are quick to target organized religion as a sinister culprit in human affairs. Chain a monster and it will attack. Like the monstrous Dracula who only came out in the darkness, much of Hollywood is frightened by the *cross*.

Art is a good thing. Art is a reflection of Truth, and is therefore a "God thing" as well. But when monstrous artists birth their hideous progeny on the public, we need to *cross*-examine this art. The value of art needs to be subordinate to the value of mankind. We must celebrate art that inspires and avoid art that demeans. The great tragedy of this "endarkenment" approach to art has been the senseless devaluation and neglect of true masterpieces. For there is no sonnet nor song, no painting nor picture, that can ever equal the intrinsic worth of a single human being. No play can equal the wonder of a child at play. No manuscript can compare to the dignity of a man. Each of us is a priceless masterpiece fashioned from The Master's hand.

The end of all music should be the glory of God and the refreshment of the human spirit.

J.S. BACH

Eden

My grace is sufficient for you, for power is made perfect in weakness. 2 Corinthians 1:9

Paradise found. One man and one woman walked in blissful Eden, a state of human joy with no human suffering — no illness, no disease, no hate, no death — until their sin banished them from Eden's gate, never to return. Paradise lost.

It would be difficult to find a person in the world who is not familiar with this story. We all remember Adam, Eve, the serpent, the forbidden fruit, the choice, the consequence. But what about the flaming sword? What about the cherubim? God places a cherubim, whom many forget in the story of Eden, as a sentry, holding a revolving flaming sword that spins fire upon anyone who dares try to re-enter the garden. The message of the cherubim is clear. *We cannot get back into the garden!* Perhaps our unfamiliarity with the cherubim's role is not without reason. According to psychiatrist and author M. Scott Peck, unable to accept real life — a desert wilderness filled with *both* human joy and human suffering — we still try desperately to penetrate an impenetrable barrier between ourselves and perfect human happiness. We forget the cherubim and seek to get back into an Eden that is forever lost.

Life is difficult. It is also wonderful. Rarely do people have a hard time accepting the *wonderful* aspects of life. However, psychologists say that our inability to accept the *difficulties* of life lies at the root of much of our problems. Neurosis is always an excuse for legitimate suffering. Centuries before science made

110

this insight, an enlightened Siddartha Gautama, the Buddha, identified suffering as the root cause of human darkness. Can we accept that for the rest of our lives, day in and day out, we will suffer? This challenge confronts us all.

Despite the truth of the Genesis story, there are many in our world who propose ways to return to Eden. One such example of this are the modern day alchemists who create elixirs that try to offer secret entry back to the garden — a deadly illusion. Just as medieval alchemists searched in vain for a potion that could offer immortality, the abuse of drugs vainly promises an escape from difficult reality. And no drug is offered for this purpose more than alcohol. I am speaking here not about the *use* of alcohol, but rather of its *abuse*. The main motivation for the abuse of alcohol is to escape reality, to return to Eden. Alcohol's numbing effect is pleasurable. That's why we get drunk. Yet every action we take has an equal and opposite spiritual reaction inside us. In drunkenness, we don't escape reality, only our humanity. We had only drugged ourselves into believing we had escaped it, making "the morning after" that much harder to accept.

Sometimes adolescents exemplify problems that adults hide more subtly. As a high school teacher, I have seen young people abuse alcohol as a "social lubricant" to reveal emotions concealed when sober, or as "liquid courage" to provide a false sense of confidence they lack when sober. Everyone can relate to a young lad nervously trying to approach a pretty girl. Like Popeye in need of spinach-induced strength, alcohol-induced confidence is an attractive choice for an awkward youth. After a few drinks, his jokes seem more amusing and he feels infinitely more charming than he really is. With each drinking episode, it is easier for him to prefer this chemical brand of confidence over sober self-consciousness. Using alcohol as a coping mechanism, instead of developing this ability within, stagnates real growth — arrested development. A pleasurable "high" is attractive, then addictive, and potentially enslaving.

These are the same teens who, ten years earlier, could amuse themselves for hours with a few simple toys. They brought creativity to life, rather than siphon pleasure from it. They now require alcohol to have a "good" time. What happened to them? They followed adult example, and they have imitated us well. The childlike spark that created an inner attitude of courage to transform reality, has been replaced by the childish escape from reality through beer, which "lowers" their mind by an ironic "high." Beer is stimulating; they no longer are. They have learned to manipulate their environment chemically and have unlearned how to master their attitude spiritually. Our pleasure-first culture has taught them the way to a "better" life through chemicals. Of course, they say they don't *need* to abuse alcohol, they only *want* to. But they are willing to lie to parents they supposedly love, harm a body they supposedly respect, break the law of a country they supposedly honor, and wrong their relationship with Christ whom they supposedly adore — sounds like *need* to me. Children learn well from their elders.

I do not mean to overly criticize the adolescent problem of alcohol abuse. I cite it here only to illustrate a deeper problem our culture exhibits towards escaping the difficulties that life brings. To promote "escape" is to create a culture of cowardice. To promote "escape" is to promote adultery — unfaithfulness to the sanctity of life no matter how difficult life may be, in sickness and in health, for better or for worse. Excessive distilled "spirits" are far from spiritual. In our culture and in ourselves, our ultimate allegiance must go either to Jesus Christ or Jack Daniels, for as Jesus reminded us, no slave can serve two masters.

This is not to imply that alcohol is not good. It is more than good, it can even be sacred. Our Lord chose wine to be the vessel of His blood. Beer is one gift from God I gladly receive, but when playing with liquid fire, caution is required. It's easy for a husband or wife to relate to a few drinks after a hard day at the office, rather than to each other. It's seductively attractive for a parent to deal another drink to herself rather than deal with her children. The slide from use to abuse can be a slippery slope. What was once a blessing can become a curse. Rather than possessing alcohol as a good, it is easy for alcohol to begin to possess us for no good at all.

The moral principle of justice — giving each person their due — demands that we are responsible, meaning "able to respond." When drunk, a person's judgment, balance, coordination, and perception are impaired by the ether-effect of the liquid sedative. God wills us to grow, not regress. Acceptance of suffering offers us a solution to the problem of Eden.

We can accept the desert wilderness that is life, and build *the Kingdom* within the desert. The path to the Kingdom of God is paved with legitimate suffering. Like Christ did, we can accept joy when it finds us and embrace it, and when suffering finds us, we can accept and embrace it as well. We can find a meaning in suffering that gives us the courage to bear it. The lessons learned from the school of suffering graduate to joy. God is shaping us for bigger things; shaping us with suffering's anvil. Christ on the cross is the way through pain to promise, through suffering to joy, through death to life. When we breach the barrier of death through Christ who walked with us on our path of suffering, we will have the last laugh. For hiding within our pain all along was a secret friend, known as… *joy.*

❧

The deeper that sorrow carves into your being,
the more joy you can contain. Is not the cup
that holds your wine the very cup that
was burned in the potter's oven?

KAHLIL GIBRAN

113

Aliens

*But the serpent said to the woman: "You certainly will
not die! No, God knows well that the moment you eat of
it your eyes will be opened and you will be like God."*

Genesis 3:4-5

The X-files have been found.
They are in a not-so-secret document known as the Gospels.
The "X" stands for Christ, and He has the answers we seek.

Public fascination with life on other planets is a cyclical
phenomenon. For decades, little can be heard about the quest
to discover extraterrestrial life. Yet, at other times, the interest
becomes overwhelming. Such is the case now, as we enter the
new millennium.

From a purely scientific point of view, it is very reasonable
to seek life on other planets. It's a big universe out there and it
is possible that we are not the only planet to sustain biological
life. Scientific exploration may also reveal secrets about our own
Earth and its origins. For these reasons alone, Catholics can join
in the enthusiasm for a star trek quest for knowledge with an
eager heart and mind. But running parallel to this reasoned endeavor has been an increasing fascination with U.F.O.'s and alien
beings, sort of a Roswell-mania that has moved the paranormal
to the level of the abnormal. Television series, blockbuster movies, Internet sites, bestselling books, and syndicated radio talks
shows abound with alleged extraterrestrial fact and fiction.

Although no one will use the word, due to political correctness in our ever-secular society, the zeal is nothing short of "religious." This isn't so surprising. As society marginalizes traditional organized religion with its difficult moral laws and inflexible dogmas, it provides little guidance to the spiritual questions of human existence. And human nature abhors a vacuum. So we see a "new religion" springing forth — an old wolf that has been tried, found lacking, and forgotten centuries ago, in new sheep's clothing. Perhaps its Jerusalem is Roswell, its scripture is the X-files, its Pontius Pilate is government conspiracy, and its Savior is an alien or alien race yet to make its public appearance. And, providing it is careful and never uses terms like "religion" or "dogma," it is a "religion" that can flourish and a "dogma" that can be promulgated.

It is not my purpose here to attack "u.f.o.logy" and show its obvious flaws. It will fall on its own contradictions and failures, only to resurface again sometime in the future, without me needing to give it a push. What is interesting is the longing for spiritual answers that this folly reveals. Hidden within a language of scientific speculation is a *religious* hope that "we are not alone" in the universe — that somewhere "out there" lies someone who can provide something of an answer to our deepest spiritual needs. Alas, they are looking for God in all the wrong places.

This pseudo-scientific movement can at best only give us speculation and hope for a desire which *faith* has already satisfied! The religious person already knows we are not alone, and we have already made first contact. For us to reach the Ultimate Life, God, we don't have to bridge a physical gap of time and space as some Stargazers might think, but a spiritual gap of pride, fear, and hate as some Stargazers might fear. God is the solution to our aloneness and He has given us each other. We are *not* alone in the universe; we never have been, we never will be.

And what do the Stargazers hope for from this alien super-race? Perhaps they could reveal scientific secrets to end hunger, hate, and homelessness in our world. But we already have promising scientific solutions. America's agricultural storehouses could feed the world. America's architectural genius could shelter the masses. But the problem goes far deeper than science. We can build houses for bodies but we cannot provide homes for souls. We produce grain for hunger but no food satisfies the hunger of the heart.

What we truly want this alien life to reveal, therefore, is a way out of our own human weakness and frailty. Then our search for alien life has ended. The alien has landed. We are the *aliens*! Though originally united to God and to ourselves, we wanted more. We wanted to *be* God. Through the sin of pride, our rebellion from God caused us to become *alien*ated from ourselves. We were *one*, but now split in two — spirit in conflict with nature, soul discordant with body, love rivaled by sin. As Adam and Eve became separated from God, the next step in this horrid regression was when Cain became separated from Abel. *Alien*ated, man became an alien nation — *alien*ated from each other. Estranged from God our Father, we stopped seeing others as our brothers and sisters. Here is where we see the folly of those who have turned the quest for extraterrestrials into a "religion." They, like all of us, exist as spiritual orphans, seeking a "brother" from the world beyond yet forgetting the one that lives next door. The *alien* we would encounter would turn out to be a fellow orphan, when what we need is a Father to make us a human family again.

We see signs of this *alien*ation in the "*alien* nation" around us. Nations pass laws to save whales but allow the killing of unborn males and females. Protesters cry for animal rights yet barely a tear is shed for countless human wrongs. Sex, once sacred, is marketed as a secular medium of exchange while money has become sacred. Meanwhile the "reel world" is distorting our picture of the "real world." People grieve the death of a celebrity they had never met, while they ignore the death of a neighbor they never bothered to meet. We have "virtual" relationships instead of authentic ones. Truth, our former master, has become our servant as lying, cheating, and stealing become commonplace. Time, our former servant, has become our master as everyone seems to be in such a hurry. The human race can easily degenerate into a rat race. And we are in such a hurry to win that we forget that the winner of a rat race is still a rat. We race faster, but fewer runners understand why we are racing. Shakespeare understood our fundamental flaw when he penned these words, speaking through the character of Julius Caesar,

The fault, dear Brutus, lies not in the stars but in ourselves.

But our Stargazer friends are not as far off as we might think. The answer does lie in the stars. In fact, I recall a story of three such Stargazers from the East. They were wise men indeed, for unlike modern men, they found the answer to the riddle of the cosmos in a child, a baby lying in a manger. They found not life on Mars, the god of war, but life in the Christ-child, the God of love.

For those of us in search of a Superman from a far away planet, there is good news to share. He has already come. He has defeated sin, evil, and death, and He wishes to make us into supermen, *Christ*ian-men, as well. He has left our planet a wonderful gift — gift that is food for our deepest hunger, that is love for our most brutal hate, and home for our wayfarer heart — the gift of Himself.

Although humanity is *alien*ated, Christ can make us whole. Just as divinity and humanity were one in Him, He can begin to make us one, once again. For before humanity became an *alien*, we were in *union*. Before we fell and became an *alien* nation, we were a family. Before we were homeless, we were *Home*. Before *original sin*, there was *original grace*. Before Genesis reminded us that we are dust and unto dust we shall return, Genesis proclaimed we were made in the image and likeness of God, and into God's likeness we can return. Although our *alien* battle will never be over in this life, with Christ, it will be won in our death. Death, once the horrific consequence of sinful *alien*ation, has been transformed by Christ into glory. Jesus gave us a glimpse of this final transfigured promise in His resurrection.

For those of us who have chosen a close encounter of the Christ-kind, we must always remember:

The search for home begins in the eyes of a homeless man.
The hunger for new life will be filled in food for the hungry.
The alien life we seek is as near as our estranged neighbor.
The longing to reach for the stars begins with prayer on our knees.

The answers to the mysteries of man are found not in matter but in a *Man*. God remains, as distant as a supernova, and as close as the nearest heartbeat.

> *Spirit and Nature have quarreled in us;*
> *that is our disease.*
>
> C.S. LEWIS

Robin Hood

They will fight with the Lamb, but the Lamb will con-
quer them, for he is Lord of lords and King of kings, and
those with him are called, chosen, and faithful.

Revelation 17:14

Megabyte mail and instantaneous faxes, concrete edifices and
Styrofoam packing material — we live in a hectic world. But
sometimes, my mind recalls a legendary heroic past complete
with rich green forests and damsels in distress. Robin Hood of
the 12th century was the quintessential hero — fighting with his
band of merry men in Sherwood Forest, taking from the rich and
giving to the poor; a marksman with a bow, and dueling with
the evil Sheriff of Nottingham. How much of this legend is fact
or fiction, I don't much care — it is the stuff that great stories
are made of. But alas, the days of kingdoms, knights, and chiv-
alry exist only in a mythic past. Robin Hood is dead.

Or is he?

The legend of Robin Hood harkens back to a time of "the
divine right of kings." Since nature exists as a hierarchy of being
— man, animals, plants, etc., people assumed that *human* nature must exist as a hierarchy as well. Royal families like the
Hapsburgs, Tudors, and Romanovs dominated the landscape of
Western European history, with men and women dedicating
their lives in service to their king. Robin Hood himself was loyal
to King Richard the Lionhearted, whose throne had been
usurped by Prince John.

Then came the Renaissance, when the ordinary man stood up and challenged the time-honored assumption of "people supremacy." Democracy was born — the belief that the Creator endows all men with fundamental rights and dignity. Among free men, there should be no kings and queens. A title such as "Princess Diana" was thought to be deceptive because her title was derived from a false kingship. All women can claim the title of princess, for each was thought to be an equal daughter to the Creator. This democratic ideal spread to every village and hamlet, and across the Atlantic Ocean. Tea was dumped in Boston harbor and a shot was heard around the world. The great American experiment began, and still continues throughout the world. And legends such as Robin Hood became nothing more than an antiquated story, suitable only for a child's nursery.

Democracy may have been born in Greece, but it was conceived long before that. Genesis proclaims the democratic equality of all humanity. The woman was created out of Adam's rib — not out of his head to rule him, nor out of his foot to be trampled on, but out of his rib to be side by side with him. We are all equally in service before our Maker. The democratic ideal proclaims that no one is better or worse than any one else. God's unconditional love is bestowed upon all without prejudice. We are significant, not because of what we do, but because of who we are. This egalitarianism is not an equality of gifts or holiness. The Pope, for example, possesses a tremendous intellect and a great holiness. His spiritual gifts are inspiring. For his authoritative role and his personal witness to Christ, he can be admired and respected. But in terms of his intrinsic value, he is no better or worse than any other in God's eyes. All humanity is wrapped in the unconditional love of God.

However, in their zeal to affirm this basic human equality, the "enlightenment" of the 16th century began to "throw the baby out with the bath water." In their passion to dethrone human sovereignties throughout the world, they rejected the one *true* monarchy beyond the world. They forgot that there is one Royal Family. God is the real King of Kings, Jesus is the true Prince of Peace, and Mary is Queen of the Angels. Christians are knights of the celestial roundtable. When history turned its back on the rightful King of Kings, rival claims to superiority began to emerge that attacked the democratic ideal. Two such claims are *cultural elitism* and *historical elitism.*

Holding up an individual or group as having superior rights or status is the *cultural elitism* of aristocracy. Even in America with its constitutionally declared equality there exists the "cult of the celebrity." We see this in our perception of actors, musicians, and athletes. Consider, for example, how crowds will stand for hours outside the entrance to the Oscar ceremony, hoping just to catch a glimpse of Hollywood stars adorned in their royal accouterments. Our moral capacity to reasonably judge ideas and actions can get suspended as we gaze in awe at the "beautiful people." Rock stars defy laws on stage and get away with degradation and obscenity in their music, yet fans still clamor just to touch them. Corporations that pollute streams will receive more protest than rockers that pollute young peoples' minds. Even my home city of Cleveland has built a Rock & Roll Hall of Fame (or for some inductees, should it be "Hall of Shame?") to immortalize musicians whose lyrics and manner openly advocated promiscuity, drug abuse, or violence, without enshrining even a word of ethical criticism. The rock counterculture is now in mainstream culture. Millionaire athletes are also given latitude of behavior that no ordinary person enjoys. How many professional athletes have we heard about who have assaulted fans and openly promoted or been guilty of casual sex, immodesty, drug use, wife abuse, and still magazines fight to have their pictures on the cover. Meanwhile, dazzled, impressionable children admire and imitate them.

Clearly, actors, artists, and athletes deserve respect for their respective talents. But they often enjoy a kingly status above plumbers, teachers, nurses, and scientists. False nobility has claimed a throne. We are in need of a Robin Hood.

Another form of intellectual superiority demonstrated by the present generation comes in its treatment of the past. An *historical elitism* reigns in the minds of many, believing that those who lived before us were inferior and ignorant. Historical elitists believe that man is spiritually and morally evolving, which makes the ideas of today sovereign over the ideas of yesterday. Past civilizations are seen as morally or spiritually "primitive," despite the obvious barbarism of our own century. People are as potentially primitive now as they always have been. British reporters once asked Mahatma Gandhi the question, "What do you think of Western civilization?" Gandhi replied, "I think that would be a good idea." Our hearts are no more "civil" now than they have always been. The Catholic Church grasps this truth, and places a value on tradition. As G.K. Chesterton explained, "tradition is the democracy of the dead." We listen to the voice of everyone and not only the voice of the living. We assert the value of all men and women, living and dead, who play a part in God's kingdom. We fight the historical elitism that can negatively influence the value we place on past ideas and individuals. When the intellectual tyranny of the living arises, we are in need of a Robin Hood.

Even though the form of history changes, the substance remains the same. There will always be, spawning out of sinful hearts, persons claiming superiority and power. And just as true, there will always be, springing from loving hearts, persons upholding justice and service. Spiritual heroes and villains will always be around, no matter how many computers there are. There is a Robin Hood within everyone, as well as an evil Sheriff of Nottingham. The battle will rage throughout history because the battle rages inside our hearts. That is why communities dedicated to the democratic ideal among men, and the royalty of God, are so important. Catholics, both Mary-men and merry men, will always rally to produce and to support the Robin Hoods of this world. We will rise to counter any rival claims to the sovereignty of God and the equality of man.

By recognizing the value of all that has gone before us, we can be *conservative in the faith* of our forefathers. Holding fast to our one, true Lord, *Jesus the Lionhearted*, will help us see the spark of royal blood in each of us. Recognizing the intrinsic worth of all who are with us, we can be *liberal in the love* we bestow on our brothers and sisters. Loving service, not sinful superiority, will create an acceptance of the democratic ideal and only then can God's love heal and transform our land.

> *Love, properly applied, is the best SAT prep course available. Any good teacher would prefer a student who knows she is loved to one who knows her ABC's.*
> *Love, given and received, will empty our prisons.*
> *Love, passing the test of time, will reduce our need for lawyers, doctors, social workers, and psychologists.*
> *Love, freely borne, will save us, for even as we give it to them, we will receive even more.*
> *Love, like all gifts, can only be given if we first have it towards our God and ourselves. Only a true Christian can give Christ.*

For every Goliath, there will be a David. For every Grendel, there will be a Beowolf. For every evil dragon, there will be a St. George. For every dangerous green knight, there will be a Sir Gawain. And for every usurper of the divine throne of Christ, out of an emerald forest armed with a bow in one hand and a crucifix in the other, there will always be a Robin Hood.

❧

Democracy cannot be saved by supermen, but only by the unswerving devotion and goodness of little men.
ADLAI STEVENSON

123

Part Three:

THE CENTER OF THE CROSS
The Mystery of Jesus and Our Relationship to Christ

THE WAY OF DISCIPLESHIP

Title	*Theme*
1. Superman	Myth and Truth
2. The Key	Salvation
3. The Lion	Jesus the Man
4. Apples	Jesus the Teacher
5. Tin Man	Conversion
6. Charlie Brown	Sin
7. Wood Winds	Crucifixion
8. Eagles	Resurrection
9. Santa Claus	Resurrection and Saints
10. Pez	Nature of Jesus
11. Triple Play	Trinity
12. Crossroads	Call To Decision

Superman

> *For to us a child is born, to us a son is given... and his name shall be called "Wonderful Counselor, Mighty God, Everlasting Father, Prince of Peace."* Isaiah 9:6

This is the tale of two Supermen and the truth about *the* Superman. The first two are alive only as words of their creators, the last is truly alive and is the Word of the Creator.

At the turn of the century in Germany, in an intellectual ivory tower there lived a timid, syphilitic professor named Friedrich Nietzsche. He created a fictional ideal and named him Zarathustra. He would be the "Ubermench," the Superman, a man who would crush the weak and enable the strong. He would lead the common folk of the 20th century, for he would heroically face the truth... that God is dead and we have killed him. He would accept a meaningless universe, reject reason, and would leap over moral standards in a single bound. Nihilism, the inherent worthlessness of reality, would reign supreme. The Superman would be his own god, with a will to power, not service. And so, on the pages of a tragic book, this Dr. Frankenstein gave birth to his fictional monster.

Less than thirty years later, all this was read by a failed artist in a jail cell, who longed to make this story a reality. This short, mustached man saw himself as the Superman, and he would build a race of Aryan supermen. His name was Adolph Hitler. Nietzsche's dream had come true, and it was a nightmare. The monster had become a man.

During those same 1930's, in a neighborhood of Cleveland, Ohio in the U.S.A., there lived two young artists named Jerry Siegel and Joe Shuster. They created their own fictional ideal and named him Clark Kent. He, too, would be an "Ubermench," a Man of Steel, but he would use his strength to protect the weak. He would live with the common folk of his country and embrace their beliefs that life was meaningful and all should strive for moral goodness. And so, on the pages of a comic book, two Americans gave birth to a fictional super hero. Superman was born:

- He was sent from another world, the planet Krypton, by a loving Father.
- He grew up in Smallville, under the care of adoptive parents.
- He learned that his powers were to be used for service, not for personal gain.
- He came to realize his special mission to save the people of Earth.
- Upon reaching adulthood, he began his public mission as Superman.
- He maintained a secret identity as Clark Kent, newspaper reporter.
- He performed wondrous deeds far beyond those of mortal man.
- He had X-ray vision.
- He had telescopic vision to see what was far away.
- As Clark Kent, he was humble and mild mannered.
- He would retreat to his "Fortress of Solitude" in the Arctic.
- He was a man of his people, the American dream come true.
- He would fight for truth and justice in the big city metropolis.
- He worked with other Super Heroes in the Justice League of America.
- Though opposed by the forces of evil, his goodness would triumph in the end.

Like any good myth, Superman was the embodiment of America's hopes and dreams of the 1930's. We were a country facing the threats of the emerging metropolis. As Paul Bunyan had conquered the feared rivers of the pioneers, as Pecos Bill had lassoed the tornadoes that plagued the Midwest, as John Henry had defeated the machine, the power of the Industrial Age, so Superman reigned over the Metropolis, able to leap tall buildings in a single bound and outrun speeding bullets.

But good mythology can embody hopes far deeper than mere social concern. The fear of death, disease, sin, and evil transcend culture and speak to the entire human condition. These deepest dreams have been translated into myths, legends, and fantasies by countless cultures. They express the hope that someday a *real* Superman will come to destroy evil, to cure disease, to conquer sin, and to transform death. Well, I have good news to bring. Superman is here.

The dream has come true.
The ideal has become real.
The story has become history.
The myth has become matter.
The Master has become man.

Fact and fiction have merged. Fantasy and reality have met. Words made of ink have been replaced by the Word made flesh. He is here. He has been here. Have we noticed? Or have we been asleep? And what kind of dreams have we nurtured — hopeful daydreams or horrid nightmares? We must be careful what we wish, for sometimes dreams come true. And the greatest one has.

This is the extraordinary claim of Christianity. But we proclaim not a Superman of human design, as is the comic Caped Crusader, but a Superman of divine design, for the real Superman can not be controlled by our desires. The divine Author of the human drama, out of love, chose to become a character in

"His" story. Only God could defeat a supernatural foe, and only a man could redeem mankind. So God became a man of flesh in actual history. It was a role only He could play. *Jesus* is the Superman.

- He came from beyond this world, sent by His loving heavenly Father.
- He was raised in a small town under the holy care of His mother and adopted father.
- Despite desert temptations, He learned that his powers were for service, not for personal gain.
- He accepted his personal mission to save the people of Earth from the slavery of sin.
- Upon reaching adulthood, He began his public mission as the Son of God.
- He kept His identity secret, but slowly revealed it as our faith grew.
- He performed miraculous deeds far beyond those of mortal men.
- He had X-ray vision to see through to our hearts.
- He had a telescopic vision of the future Kingdom of God.
- He was a humble and mild mannered Superman, for He saw gentleness as strength.
- He constantly retreated to His inner "fortress of solitude" in prayer to His Father.
- He was a man of His people, a Jewish reformer, their messianic dream come true.
- He was Truth and Justice, which He proclaimed everywhere, including the big city of Jerusalem.
- He gathered disciples — a "justice league" to protect the weak and feed the hungry.
- Though opposed by the forces of evil, His Godliness triumphed in the end.

Superman

Lex Luthors of the world, beware! The *real* Superman is here. Even the "kryptonic" rock which entombed Him could not defeat Him, for He rolled the stone away and rose from the dead. Those who saw the resurrected Christ were willing to proclaim this super-fact at the cost of their lives. Their martyred blood validates their amazing testimony as authentic. And the dream come true continues today. There are many Lois Lanes and Jimmy Olsens seeking daily to better the planet, reporting the good news to every small town and huge metropolis, fighting for truth, justice and the sometimes un-American way. His disciples bear the mark of the Savior and Son, the "S" on their hearts. His mark, seen only by the eyes of faith, is missed by those who choose to see only with their eyes. But their secret identity can be revealed and His mark of love can be seen on many different souls, such as on a "crazy" man of Assisi, on a peasant girl of Lourdes, or on a holy man of Rome.

Jesus: the Jewish dream fulfilled, the American dream (at its best) answered, and the Nietzschean nightmare destroyed. Jesus Christ is the Superman. He can truly be called the "Man of Steal," for He has stolen our sins away.

●

"These are the amazing attributes which SUPERMAN, savior of the helpless and oppressed, avails himself as he battles the forces of evil and injustice."
SIEGEL AND SHUSTER, 1940

131

The Key

I will place the key of the House of David on his shoulder; when he opens, no one shall shut, when he shuts, no one shall open.   Isaiah 22:22

There is a warmth and a light to childhood. But each of us faces a chilling challenge in our adulthood. We must solve the riddle of human happiness. Consider the mystery of "The Castle and the Key."

Having left home, you find yourself in a cold and unsheltered land. Ahead of you there stands a single castle on a hill. Drawing closer to it, you see its only door, made of a thick mahogany wood, showing only a keyhole. The door is locked from the outside in, but open from the inside out, and is impenetrable by force. You stand outside the castle in the frozen world. Peering through a leaded glass window, you see a warm fire raging in the fireplace. Two leather chairs face the hearth and two glasses of a deep, dark, burgundy wine have been placed on a table between them. One chair appears to be occupied by the owner of the castle, but you cannot see His face. The other chair bears an inscription, and to your surprise, you read your name on it. Suddenly, it is clear what you must do. The only way into the castle is by *possessing the golden key* that unlocks the door. In a sense, the *key must control you*, for a key is made for a particular purpose, and a key must be used as it is intended in order to open a door.

But you are not alone in the cold. Amidst the darkness and swirl of snow that surrounds you, you see and hear ghostly images, which sometimes seem as numerous as the snowflakes themselves, and they offer you solutions to your human misery. One such ghost calls herself a materialist. She believes that you should be happy in the frozen world that surrounds you, because that is all that there is. The castle is an illusion, it doesn't really exist. A second ghost, a Marxist atheist, rejects the need for a key as a sign of weakness. He relies solely on himself, not keys, to get through locked doors. A third ghost, raised religious but not practicing any particular religion, explains that it doesn't matter which key you have. As long as you have a key, any will do. Another ghost of great intellect lectures that having the key is not important. You need only to intellectually acknowledge the reality of the key to get through the locked door. To make matters even more confusing, a fifth ghost, a theologian, professes that in order to get through the locked door, you should study the history and metaphysical nature of keys rather than having the key. Still another "new age" ghost tells you that if you rely on your inner spiritual energy, you can transform yourself into the key that you need. You hear yet a seventh ghost, a psychologist, state that keys are illusions, created by your mind due to your subconscious desire to get through the door. Finally, a playboy ghost laughs aloud and declares freely that the door is the gold you should desire; not the castle, not the fireplace, and certainly not the mysterious stranger who will be sitting next to you in His chair.

Each of us must decide which way will lead to true happiness. But along the path of our life, we hear many voices. We must solve the mystery of *"The Castle and the Key."* Here is the Christian solution.

> *Heaven* is the castle.
> *Life* is the dark, cold world.
> The *door* is sin, evil, and death.
> *Jesus Christ* is the golden key.

This is the faith of the New Testament. This is the clear voice of Catholic Christianity. We believe that Christ is the only way to salvation. Only God can pierce through the barrier of sin and death and conquer it. Only a perfect Man can defeat a man-made barrier perfectly. It took Someone on the "inside" to come "outside" to help us get "inside" — Someone who knows the barrier better than we do because He was never defeated by it. Though other philosophies, persons, or rituals propose to be the key, there is only one. Similar-looking keys, such as Buddha or Mohammed, will not open the door. This is not to say that there is no value to these great men and their teaching. Other religious leaders have had great insights into the way of salvation. But that is not what Christianity claims about Jesus. We do not claim Him to have discovered the way, as is professed in Taoism, we claim that Jesus *is* the *Way*. We do not claim that Jesus had a revelation from God, as does Islam, we claim that Jesus *is* the *Revelation* of God. Thomas Aquinas understood this:

> *If, then, you are looking for the way by which you should go, take Christ, because he himself is the way.*

This simple message can be lost to even Christians themselves, who hear a myriad of different voices, both secular and religious, throughout their lives. Yet each of these voices needs always to be compared with the original voice of biblical Christianity as it is articulated by the Catholic Church. This one voice continually tells us that we cannot reach Heaven by studying Christ or by talking about Him. We can't even get there by intellectual belief alone. We can't arrive by earning heaven through certain deeds or rituals. We get there by *possessing Christ* inside, and, more importantly, by *Christ possessing us inside of Him*. It requires the twofold assent of faith and surrender of love. Jesus is *the Master Key* that unlocks the secret of life. It's that simple. What is not simple is knowing who does or does not ultimately possess Christ. That's a judgment that can only be made by God. A non-Christian can know Christ in his *heart* without knowing Him in his head. Theologian Karl Rahner called this the "anonymous Christian." On the other hand, a professed Christian might say she believes in Jesus, yet in her thoughts and deeds she rejects Christ. So the question "Who possesses Christ?" needs to be turned inward and asked: "Do *I* possess Christ?" Christians are persons who have said "Yes" to Christ possessing them, in faith and love. The theological virtues of faith and love are two sides of the same coin. Faith is love's invisible roots. Love is faith made visible. To love someone is to be faithful to them.

I have met many Christians who still think that eternal life is determined by the adding up of our good actions and then subtracting our bad actions. If we did more "goods" than "bads," we go to Heaven. If we did more "bads" than "goods," we go to Hell. Sort of like a spiritual board game; "Do not pass Go, Do not collect $200." We have created a legalistic religion, visioning God as a stern judge rather than a loving Father, trying to "earn" our salvation by living a good life. I know of no Christian today who can say that he or she has lived a good life. At best, we can only live a "somewhat" good life. We all throw an errant pitch, which ruins our "perfect game." Christianity means looking beyond the law to the Lawmaker. Beyond the rules to the Ruler. Beyond the manner to the Man. The Catholic creed is the beginning, not the end, of faith. Dogma is the instruction manual that comes with the key. Dogma is important because it directs the use of the Key in its right way. But dogma is not the Key. *Christ* is the Key. Christ in us will unlock Heaven's castle door.

When examining closely a key and a keyhole, we find that the key fills the space inside the lock perfectly. The key is the opposite of the lock. So too, Jesus is the opposite of the barrier which prevents us from salvation, namely: sin, evil, and death. Jesus was like us in all things but sin, never was defeated by evil (though tempted), and rose from the dead. The more we abide in Him and He in us, the more we become the opposite of our sinful nature. And we too can rise with Christ someday. This is our hope. Jesus is *"the Key"* to the problem of human existence.

As keepers of the key, we share His Spirit, becoming members of His body and other Christs. And when we reach the castle door after our joyful journey, our Key will take us into the warmth of His hearth and heart. We will find that the Owner, still saving us a chair in His castle, is no stranger. We have traveled far in our journey of life, only to discover it was our Father waiting for us at the fireplace all along. An embrace welcomes us, along with a chalice of wine filled with the flavor of infinite love. A banquet has been prepared in our honor in the castle family room. *The* festival of family and friends is about to begin. Our journey which seemed long and arduous, which began at home, has brought us full circle.

We hadn't left home; we had found it, once and for all.

There was a boy who used to sit in the twilight and listen to his great aunt's stories. She told him that if he could reach the place where the end of the rainbow stands he would find there a golden key.

GEORGE MACDONALD, "THE GOLDEN KEY"

The Lion

Weep not, the Lion of the tribe of Judah, the Root of David, has conquered.   Revelation 5:5

Know thyself. This was the challenge of Socrates, one of the great teachers in history. But Socrates saw this as an ongoing process, not a quick task. There is much of man that is mystery. This is even more true of Jesus, being both human and divine. Yet the challenge remains for the Christian, because the more we *know Christ*, a perfect human, the more we can know and become ourselves. Although we can't know everything about Jesus' humanity, we can know something, and it is enough for us to begin a relationship with Him. Since images can be more powerful than ideas, consider a less used image for Jesus the Man, in relation to a familiar one.

Jesus as the *Lamb of God* is strong metaphor. It speaks to the sacrifice that God made for us. But what about the sacrifice that we must make for God? Here, another metaphor, from the book of Revelation, can assist. Jesus is the *Lion of God*, and He asks for the *lion's share* from us.

The historical Jesus was both the *Lamb* and the *Lion*; as gentle as a lamb to a faithful child, yet as forceful as a lion to a faithless Pharisee. Jesus spoke of the "lilies of the field" to comfort the afflicted, yet He spoke of the "fires of Gehenna" to afflict the comforted. Jesus healed the lame, gave sight to the blind, made the deaf hear, and spoke of a Father's forgiveness and love so divine that we should never forget. Yet He drove the moneychangers from the Temple in righteous anger, and spoke of sin, hell, damnation, and Satan more often than we would care to remember. Jesus shed tears for His friend Lazarus who had been humbled by death, yet He rebuked His friend Peter when he spoke out of pride. Jesus refused personal judgment on a prostitute and saved her from stoning with the words "let he who is without sin cast the first stone." Yet He judged her action to save her from evil with the words "go and sin no more."

The lion's majestic features and powerful strength have given it the title, the "king of beasts." It has become a symbol of strength, majesty, and courage. Jesus showed this same kingly power when, as a teacher, He spoke on His own authority. This might not seem very radical by today's standards, but consider that, in Jesus' day, it was characteristic of all rabbis, when answering a question, to quote a previous rabbi like Hillel or Gamaliel, and therefore speak on the authority of the past tradition. Not unlike today, a lawyer must cite a precedent in another case as the basis for his own claims. But Jesus broke with this tradition and spoke on His own authority, to the great consternation of the scribes and Pharisees. They saw that Jesus was not playing by the rules. This was true. Jesus did not come to live by human rules; He came to be the Ruler. *The Lion* is the Ruler, and He makes the rules.

The forcefulness of Jesus the *Lion* is best illustrated in what I have always considered a most disturbing story, that of the Rich Young Man. Here Jesus answers the question that all of us, at one time or another, have wondered: "What must I do to be saved? How can I get to heaven?" Jesus answers the rich young man bluntly. He must sell *everything* that he owns, give the money to the poor, and then come follow Christ. I'm sure the rich young man first thought that Jesus' answer was a nice metaphor, a good use of hyperbole. No! He must do *exactly* as the *Lion* has commanded. Now I don't know about others, but I own things. And I like what I own. Am I the rich young man? Yet in a similar story Jesus asks for only a percentage of Zacchaeus' wealth to be given away. Which is it? The answer lies in the kind of lion that Jesus came to be. Wherever our treasure lies, there our heart will likewise be. Whatever "pearl of great price" we cling to other than God, Jesus would call us on it. His *Lion's claw* would fiercely tear at any "false god" closest to our heart: our popularity, possessions, intellect, money, art, status, talent, physical beauty, friends, family, etc. The rich young man didn't really own his possessions; his possessions owned him. The need to turn that around was the "eye of the needle" that he needed to pass through in order to enter the Kingdom and truly say "Yes!" to the *Lion's rule*. But Jesus' challenge would be different for every person. I wonder what "false god" each of us might be clinging to right now? Consequently, His original listeners tended to either radically accept Jesus or radically reject Him. We are either in *the Lion's lair,* or we are not. And He tolerates no debate about whom we must serve.

The kind of Ruler that Jesus came to be ran counter to the expectations of the people around Him, and they still shock the world's notion of greatness. Jesus was not a politician, a military general, a corporate giant, a lawyer, a consecrated religious leader, a professional athlete, a movie star, a revolutionary, a Marxist, a world traveler, an ascetic, or a superstar. Jesus was:

a **Son**... to His earthly mother and father, and **Son of God** to His heavenly *Abba*, an Aramaic word Jesus used meaning Dad.

a **carpenter**... earning His daily fare as did His earthly father before Him.

a **teacher**... a layman, enlightening the minds of those meant for eternal life.

a **Jew**... He fulfilled the Law and the prophets and sought to reform abuses and exaggerations in His religion.

a **common man**... who enjoyed wedding feasts, laughed with friends, fasted for strength, and drank wine with meals.

a **man of prayer**... who prayed as naturally as we breathe. His
prayer was simple, intimate, and constant in His life.

a **friend**... to rich and poor, Jew and Gentile, male and female, popular or outcast (which included prostitutes,
tax collectors, lepers, Samaritans, women, children,
etc.), and to anyone who would turn to Him in forgiveness and love.

Each of these Jesus could do perfectly, for His nature was
perfect. But as imperfect as we are, we are nonetheless called
by the roar of the *Lion* to try and live as He lived: in sonship,
work, teaching, worship, community, prayer, and friendship.
This is the *lion's share* that Jesus asks of us.

A lion displays physical strength for his survival. Jesus dis-
played His spiritual strength for *our* survival, our salvation. In
His days on earth, Jesus knew the peace that comes from *faith*,
sleeping like a baby on a boat in a storm, while others were awake
in fear. Jesus felt the serenity of *hope*, promising paradise to a
crucified man on the brink of despair. Jesus performed the works
of *love*, giving Himself to healing others every day, even in the
face of their apathy. Jesus had a sense of *humor*, as when He
quoted a child's limerick to tease the serious-minded Pharisees
(Mt 11:16-17). Jesus felt the *pain* of rejection, being abandoned
by His own disciples; and the *joy* of acceptance by friends like
Martha and Mary who broke bread with Him. Jesus knew He
was never alone, and thus never feared *solitude*.

Legend has it that young lions are born dead only to come
back to life three days after birth when breathed on by their
parents. Here again we see Jesus as the *Lion* of the Father, risen
after three days from the dead. He will breathe His Spirit into
us, that we might rise as well. Will we surrender our pride to
join *the Lion's pride?*

The *Lion of Judah* is feared only by His enemies. To His
family, He is a protector and a friend, for He has removed the

thorn of death from our hand by allowing a nail in His. There is comfort in being a friend to the *Lion*. But this truth, that we can call Jesus friend, is not the most extraordinary truth of all. But the amazing thing is that Jesus, this *Lion*, this King of an often beastly people, calls *us* friend! What an honor! We, a speck in a multitudinous and vast galaxy, can be a friend to the Creator of the universe. God has raised us to join in His glory. *The Lion* will show the way. He will protect us from the cage of evil when we do His work, He will attack us when our earthly pride threatens His heavenly pride, and He will comfort us in the softness of His mane when we make Him our main strength.

"Aslan is a lion — the Lion, the great Lion... if there's anyone who can appear before Aslan without their knees knocking, they're either braver than most or else just silly."
C.S. LEWIS, *THE LION, THE WITCH, AND THE WARDROBE*

Apples

*Like golden apples in silver settings are words spoken at
the proper time.*   Proverbs 25:11

There were two trees in one garden. One gave life, the other gave
death. One sowed gentle humility, the other sowed toxic pride.
One had apples of golden union with God, the other apples of
poisonous rebellion from God, yet the apples from both trees
appeared red and delicious. This was Eden, the garden of God.
Which apple did we choose?

We chose death, pride, and rebellion — to be our own god.
We made Earth the garden of Man.

God never abandoned His garden, we had abandoned Him.
But through the blessed humility of a "New Eve" God sent His
Son to be a "New Adam," to sow the seeds of reunion. Jesus came
into a garden overgrown with weeds of sin and vines of vice, the
once-Godly garden was in great disrepair. In fact, it was beyond
our capacity to save. Separated from the God who first sowed
its life-giving seeds, who could teach us how to care for the garden, it was wrought with lethal thorns, venomous snakes, and
poison apples. And so Jesus the Master Teacher came and taught
us how to care for and expand the Garden, the Kingdom of God,
on earth.

Jesus often used short stories, drawn from ordinary life to
reveal hidden truths about the extraordinary Kingdom of God.
One purpose of these stories was to shock, tease, and bother the
listener, causing him to question further. This is exactly what
Jesus wanted.

Remember, many people who came to see Jesus wanted a show, the performance of a miracle. They believed themselves to have all the answers. But true learning always begins by asking questions. Jesus, the Master Teacher, used little stories and parables to make us rethink our usual conception of ourselves and God, to tease our mind, to capture our imagination, to undermine our self-centered complacency and create within us an attitude of wonderment, and humility. Consider these:

> In *The Father's Love* (a.k.a. The Prodigal Son, Lk 15:11-32), by Jewish law the Father should not welcome his Son because he is ritually unclean. The Father not only receives him, but overwhelms him in love, a love beyond all familial standards.
>
> In *The Lost Sheep* (Luke 15:4-5), the shepherd abandons ninety-nine to save just one. No real shepherd in his right mind would do this. In fact, they expect to lose a certain percentage of their flock. Again, the shepherd's love for that one sheep is a radical love beyond human understanding.

Can we accept a God who is not only good, but loves us beyond our wildest dreams? Some people find these "apples," these truths, so rich in the nutrients of faith, hope, and love, too luscious to bite, too good to be true. So we settle for "maybe there's a God" or "maybe there's some kind of afterlife." We settle for a bland apple whose seeds produce a halfhearted religion tree and fruit that gives us the illusion that we are in control in our garden. After all, what would those sweet golden apples of the Master Gardener do to us? Our religion would have to become "radical," a word that means "rooted." We wouldn't want to be seen as fanatics. What would the neighbors say?

Jesus the Teacher spent His days offering apples of gold whose seeds would produce a new tree of life in the garden of this world. He proclaimed that God is our loving Father, our

Abba, our Dad, who loves His children no matter how rotten to the core we might be. We need only to surrender our control over to Him. On His last day, our Teacher gave us one final lesson, a living parable, before class was dismissed. He went to the garden of olives near the Tree of Death, upon which blossomed the most poisonous apples of them all. And Jesus was nailed to that Tree and He ate of its fruit. But in the end, it was death that died. The Tree of Death was transformed into a Tree of Eternal Life. In the center of our garden this Tree still stands. It is a gateway to the Kingdom of God. Its apples are red, the color of His blood. They taste bitter to some, sweet to others, but are life-giving to all. An apple a day keeps the demon away. If we follow Him to the Tree, we too can bear fruit for the Kingdom of God.

There are two trees in our earthly garden. One gives eternal life, the other, death. One sows gentle humility, the other sows toxic pride. One has apples of golden union with God, the other apples of poisonous rebellion against God, yet the apples from both trees appear red and delicious. Which apple will we choose?

❧

And pluck till time and time are done
The silver apples of the moon,
The golden apples of the sun.
THE SONG OF THE WANDERING AENGUS

Tin Man

I came that they might have life and have it to the full.
John 10:10b

When a man's an empty kettle, he should be on his mettle,
*   and yet I'm torn apart.*
Just because I'm presumin' that I could be kind of human,
*   if I only had a heart.*

Consider the Tin Woodsman from the *Wizard of Oz*: He longed for a heart that he already had. He searched down a yellow-brick road which led to the Emerald City. He found a Wizard who could not give him what he desired — to be made human.

We are a different kind of Tin Man. We long for a heart that we don't yet have. If we search down the yellow-brick road which leads to the City of God, we can find a Wizard who can give us what we desire — to be made truly and fully human.

But writing about a word such as *heart* requires a brief word on its various meanings. When surgeons use the word, they refer to a biological blood-pumping organ. When poets use the word, they often refer to our psychological feelings and emotions. When Christians use the word *heart*, we refer philosophically to the entire person — body, soul, and spirit. We read in the New Testament that Jesus calls us to repent in order to enter the Kingdom of God. In the original Greek, the word for repentance is "metanoia" — which means not merely being sorry, but rather a total "change of heart," a complete psychic transformation of our entire being. This is the "heart transplant" that we need from the Great Surgeon to become fully human.

But while the Tin Man of Frank Baum's book *The Wonderful Wizard of Oz* eagerly awaits the transformation, we are much more like the obstinate "Tin Soldiers" of C.S. Lewis' book *Mere Christianity*, for we fight the change that can save us. In this book, Lewis provides great insight into human nature by using the analogy of a Tin Soldier. He asks us to imagine for a moment a story about a toy soldier who can become human through the power of a benevolent magical being. In reading stories like these, I had always assumed that the transformation process would be one that a tin soldier would welcome. But maybe not. More true to our human nature, Lewis imagines that if the toy soldier had lived his whole life being made of tin, he would be quite comfortable with his tin-ness. Tin would be real and certain. Tin is all he had ever known. He would like tin. When the magic strikes, he would be frightened. He would experience his tin being destroyed, being replaced by this unknown substance called flesh. He would fight the magic. He would resist the reformation process. It would seem to him that he would be dying. And, in a sense, he would be. He would be witnessing the death of his tin. Lewis puts it this way:

> *Imagine turning a tin soldier into a real little man. It would involve turning the tin into flesh. And suppose the tin soldier did not like it. He is not interested in flesh; all he sees is that the tin is being spoilt. He thinks you are killing him. He will do everything he can to prevent you.*

What the tin soldier couldn't know at that moment is what you and I already know; that flesh is better than tin. Being human has its advantages. If he allows the metamorphosis to take place, he will discover that being human is a better way of being. Rust-free flesh and blood is wonderful.

You and I are obstinate tin soldiers, in need of a heart. We have been granted a miraculous gift. If we remain in our present human nature, we will die. So God will provide the greatest miracle. If we choose, Christ will dwell in our hearts and transform us from sin-stained humans who die, to Sons of God who live forever. But, we fight the "heart-transplant" process. We fight the miracle. We are much more comfortable with earthly pleasure despite the fact that it doesn't fill us completely.

This Christ-change seems to be killing us. And, in a sense, Christ *is* killing us. He is killing our self-centered human nature and replacing it with His own nature. But because the physical nature is tangible and real to us, we cling to it and resist the presence of Christ, even though the Christ-nature can bring joy and eternal life.

Fortunately for us, God is just as stubborn as we are. He doesn't like to lose. In fact, He is incapable of it. In order to guarantee our victory, God Himself became a tin soldier to show us obstinate tin soldiers the way to become real. He became one of us. Jesus was more courageous than any lion, wiser than any scarecrow, and more loving than any tin man. The transformation was perfect in Christ, and now we too can become real. We can confidently undergo this "death" experience because Christ has conquered death. We need not be afraid anymore. In fact, like the Tin Man, by longing for this new heart more than fearing it, we have already begun the process. Let the conversion within us continue. Just don't expect the other obstinate soldiers to applaud us when the change begins. They will see us as being very foolish tin men. They may ask us to settle on mere improvement, offering us a nice can of oil to lubricate our joints. But we cannot settle for smooth-functioning tin. We are meant for something much greater. We are meant to be real. We need not even fear tears any more, they cannot rust us away.

Why doesn't everyone welcome the "change of heart" that Christ offers? Perhaps we fear the pain that a real heart might bring. As the Tin Man said, with tears in his eyes, as he was saying goodbye to his beloved Dorothy:

Now I know I have a heart, because I can feel it breaking.

But in our fear of pain, we lose an opportunity for joy. For the deeper sorrow carves into our being, the more joy we can contain. Broken hearts mend, stronger than they were before.

Perhaps for others, they look for God in all the wrong places. Wicked Witches of greed, lust, pride, etc. can cast spells that lead us off the right road. Some Tin Men follow the wrong yellow-brick roads, dazzled by Emerald Cities of Man that can never offer the joy of the City of God.

The choice is ours. Resist the change and remain in our comfortable tin, without a truly human heart, and rust away. Or undergo the most fearful and incredible change that mankind has ever experienced — a transformation of love. In giving us a truly human heart, the Wizard of Love can give us an entirely new nature, His own nature, capable of conquering death itself, which can lead us to a land truly over the rainbow. Be a tin soldier or a Christian soldier; Christ is awaiting our decision.

❧

And remember, my sentimental friend, that a heart is not judged by how much you love, but by how much you are loved by others.
THE WIZARD OF OZ (TO THE TIN MAN)

Charlie Brown

The law of the spirit, the spirit of life in Christ Jesus, has freed you from the law of sin and death.   Romans 8:12

"Good Ol' Charlie Brown... How I hate him."

This sad quote was in an early comic strip by Charles Schultz. It was said by a neighborhood boy as Charlie merely passed his way. Charlie is the perennial loser. Try as he does, he can't kick the football, he always loses the baseball game, and he never wins the heart of the little red-haired girl. We can relate to Charlie Brown. As much as Snoopy is the admirable success, Charlie Brown is the lovable failure. We are all lovable failures, for despite all our best efforts, we can't quite live the kind of life that we know we should. Beginning even from birth, a bad infection spread throughout our souls and we don't have the antidote. Although this original sin did not destroy our relationship with God, as Martin Luther believed, it did flaw our relationship with God. Sin is now part of the package. We all know there is a law of right and wrong but we continue to break it anyway. We call this failure, this bad infection, this flaw... sin. Sin is the deliberate violation of God's law, of God's love. St. Paul described it best:

We know that the law is spiritual, whereas I am weak flesh sold into the slavery of sin. I can not even understand my own actions. I do not do what I want to do but what I hate.   (Romans 7:14-15)

149

On this planet, we can't escape this alien infection and we can't destroy it by ourselves. It's part of our nature. As much as we would like to deny it, each of is Charlie Brown. And like Charlie, we believe that if we grit our teeth and try hard enough, we can transcend this disease by ourselves. But again, like Charlie, left to our own abilities, we continue to lose. We simply can't save ourselves.

Probably the biggest proof of our sinful nature is that we want to deny it. We will even deny denial. Nobody wants to admit that they fail to live up to a loving relationship with God. We live in a world that grasps at the power of the *atom*, yet has not grasped the sin of *Adam*. Consider this question: How often do people attend confession (either through the sacrament or otherwise) at church? — probably a small number. It's the most "hated" sacrament because it's painful to admit we are wrong.

It is much easier to deny our sinful nature than to find the courage to face it and its power over us. Karl Marx denied it when he proposed that if we reordered the distribution and production of goods, then social and personal utopia would exist. Sigmund Freud thought that if we resolved our past unconscious conflicts, we would reach psychological "nirvana." H.G. Wells and George Bernard Shaw believed in an advanced super-humanity that would eventually evolve beyond sin. On the other hand, G.K. Chesterton, the great Catholic journalist at the turn of the century, knew that the problem of sin could not be solved with the wave of a human wand. The solution required the intervention of our "fairy" God Father. And it certainly couldn't be wiped away by therapy or economics. When he was asked to publish an essay on the topic "What's Wrong With the World?" G.K. responded by simply writing:

Dear Sirs,
     I am.

               Sincerely Yours,
               G.K. Chesterton

Way to go Chesterton! We have met the enemy and he is us. Sin, evil, and death are the facts of human existence. Try as we might, we alone can't change this. Our kites are destroyed by kite-eating trees and we cling to our blankets. We can grit our teeth all we like, but we can't alter the inevitability of our own death. We are alienated from ourselves, like in the story of Adam and Eve, and consequently alienated from each other, as in the story of Cain and Abel. We are not "Abel" to perfectly please our perfect God. Linus observed this once when talking to his sister Lucy:

> *Charlie Brown says that brothers and sisters can learn*
> *to get along...*
> *He says they can get along the same way mature*
> *adults get along...*
> *And he says that adults can get along the same way*
> *nations get along...*
> *At this point the analogy breaks down.*

Is this depressing? Let's hope so. Only someone who is down can begin to go up. We can not be found until we realize that we are lost. There's no need for a Savior without a need to be saved. Just as the alcoholic needs to "bottom-out" before she can get help, as the patient in therapy needs to admit a problem before he can begin the healing, we need to accept that we are a loved sinner in order to begin to understand why Jesus came. Blankets or Beethoven cannot cure us, but Jesus can. He came to give us an injection of Himself to wipe out the disease within our sick soul. Then, with the ultimate Christ inside of us, we could ultimately conquer sin and death. But all this requires a realization that we are drowning in a whirlpool of sin. Only then can Jesus, the Lifeline, rescue us. With Jesus, we go from "zero" to "hero." Pop psychology proposes "I'm O.K., you're O.K." But Christianity has long ago revealed "I'm not O.K., you're not O.K., and that's O.K." Christ can make us "O.K."

Once while engaged in a lively debate with an atheist, I

offered him a chance for victory. I said to him, "I will cite three things. If you have defeated any of them, then you do not need Jesus. I will admit defeat and agree that Christianity is not for you. But if you answer all three things affirmatively, then I win and you have to reconsider Christ."

"Very well," he agreed.

"Sin? Have you stopped sinning? Or do you still fail to do what you know to be right?" I asked.

"I haven't stopped sinning," he admitted.

"Evil? Are you able to consistently resist evil thoughts and deeds?"

"Well, no," he replied.

"Death? Can you defeat death? Or are you going to be six-feet under the ground someday like the rest of us?"

"No," he conceded.

"Well I know someone who has. I think you might like to meet him. He lived 2000 years ago in Nazareth. He never sinned, He perfectly resisted evil and He rose from the dead and is living even still. Now, don't you think you owe it to yourself to at least investigate this unique and extraordinary claim?"

This is the only argument that we can win only by having lost. Or, more exactly, by *being* the lost to be found by Christ.

So take heart fellow losers of the world. There is hope. We are not alone. Remember that Jesus was seen by many as the ultimate loser, defeated on the cross, robbed of possessions, friends, and finally His life. Yet the ultimate failure is now King triumphant! All the Charlie Browns of the world have gathered together to celebrate. We call this the Church. The lost have been found. The blind can see. Losers are now winners. Charlie Brown has won a baseball game.

❧

Where sin increased, grace abounded all the more.
ROMANS 5:20

Wood Winds

Jesus cried out in a loud voice, "Father, into your hands I commend my spirit"; and when he had said this he breathed his last.   Luke 23:46

Wood is inexorably linked to life and death. A structure built of wood can shelter us or cage us. A musical instrument of wood, like a flute, must first be carved with a sharp knife in order to produce beautiful sound. A fire of wood can warm us or kill us.

Wood appears unobtrusively throughout the story of God and His people, from cedar trees of Lebanon for a magnificent Temple to the wood in the workshop of a humble carpenter:

— the wood of the Tree of Life in the Garden of Eden, giving life to those who ate of its fruit, amidst the shadow of the Tree of Death for those who chose to disobey.

— the wood of the table at the Last Supper near the Garden of Olives, giving spiritual life to those who ate at it, and despair leading to death to the one who left without partaking of the whole meal.

— the wood of the ark that preserved the life of Noah and his family at the time of the flood in which most lives were lost.

— the wood of the ark of the covenant that gave spiritual courage to the People of God when the armies of death opposed them.

— the wood of a manger that cradled the life of a newborn

baby who managed to escape Herod's slaughter of the innocents.

and most importantly of all...

— the *wood of the cross* supporting a crucified body in horrendous death, sign of the hope of resurrected life for those who follow Him to it.

For Christians, it is the *wood of the cross* that most exemplifies the apparent paradox of life through death.

At the turn of the century, the philosopher Friedrich Nietzsche proclaimed that "God is dead and we have killed him." Life, he claimed, held no hope, no truth, and no intrinsic meaning. Tragically, Nietzsche was familiar with only half the musical composition of life. Christians agree that God did die once, but His death was only the first of two related symphonic movements. The music of life's drama does contain tragic moments, but it is no tragedy. It is music for a romantic adventure with a triumphant ending. But the darkest moment in the music of life was Jesus' death, when a wooden cross stood on center stage. And only by knowing the whole story can we see how this awful symbol of death became an awesome symbol of life.

The wooden cross is *the* central symbol of Christianity. Because of its omnipresence, we can easily forget that it was, historically, an instrument of death. The Romans used crucifixion to intimidate anyone who thought of opposing their Empire. Crucifixions in Jerusalem were done regularly and visibly, seen easily by any visitor.

Jesus' crucifixion was a symphony of pain, which followed a prelude of anguish. As Adam introduced the strains of sin in the Garden of Eden, rebelling in pride against the Father's will, the New Adam changed key in the Garden of Gethsemane, accepting in humility His Father's will. Jesus was scared, as any normal human being would be anticipating a crucifixion, and yet

He remained courageous. Courage is not the absence of fear, it is the transcendence of fear. So great was His fear that the Scriptures tell us His "sweat became as drops of blood" (Lk 22:44) — a medical condition first noted by Aristotle, caused by the constriction of blood vessels near the sweat glands during times of severe stress. And His garden odyssey would end in betrayal, for only a friend can betray a friend. For thirty pieces of silver, Judas chose to dishonor Him with, of all things, a kiss. How many times in our history has the Almighty been betrayed by the "almighty dollar" and a kiss been used to kill?

Jesus' physical agony began with scourging, and it alone could easily have killed Him. The Roman soldiers used an instrument of long leather straps attached to a wooden handle, with knots in the straps containing lead or jagged pieces of bone. The straps would penetrate the skin upon impact and create a shower of blood when ripped out of the skin. Then to add insult and injury to an already brutal ordeal, a crown of thorns was jammed into His skull, resulting in severe nerve damage and a state of shock. This ended a movement of agony, but the symphony of pain was not over.

Jesus was crucified on Golgatha, the "place of skull." It was aptly named. Rats and wild dogs would roam for food amid the decaying flesh of those who died there. Jesus was stripped to highlight His helplessness and shame. Nails, nearly a foot in length, would be driven into His wrists and feet. Each blow would be a lightning bolt of torture. And then crucifixion itself, with pressure on His lungs, water building up around His heart, asphyxiation and shock, would inevitably lead to His death. Prisoners would try and use their legs to push upwards to relieve some of the immense pressure on their lungs, to take in more air. But the Romans executioners, after allowing the crucified victims to struggle to breathe and thus prolong their own agony, would finish the ordeal, using a large hammer to smash their knee caps, causing asphyxiation. When they came to do this to Jesus,

He was already dead. This was the darkest movement and the silence of death marked its painful conclusion.

Jesus' crucifixion was the culmination of His love for us. It was not demonstrated only in His death. Every day of His life He gave of Himself to others, and in giving He received. Yet this love was an affront to the hard-hearted, who wanted to lash out and attack — even crucify Him. He was too good for them. This self-emptying love reached its fullest expression on the cross, when He gave even His life for our sake.

The crucifix is the symbol of our faith. It stands bloody and horrid in the center of our churches. Not a "happy Jesus," arms raised in triumph, but a symbol of death, a death we will share. This is the fact of our existence. We cannot run from it, we cannot escape it. We are dust and unto dust we shall return. We must accept it, as Jesus did, and transcend it. We each must perform our part in the somber final passage of this movement in the symphony of our life.

Three days after His death, a new movement in the symphony began, with music more wonderful than we had ever heard, with notes more harmonious than we had ever dreamed. If we hear only the sound of His death, then Nietzsche was right, and life, as Macbeth proclaimed, is "a tale told by an idiot, full of sound and fury, signifying nothing." But deep down inside, in the darkest abyss of our being, a chord rises within us and shouts "No!" to a meaningless existence. A chant of faith, an anthem of hope, a chorus of love, begins inside each of us. And we know that the proclamation of Jesus' resurrection is real. We do not need a Shroud of Turin to know this, only a life shrouded in love. It is true to the historical facts, it is true to our own experience of life. Death, a movement of sorrow, is the prelude to a movement of resurrected joy. Jesus rose from the dead, and death no longer has its sting. He is now the conductor, wooden baton in his nail-torn hand, bringing harmony to harm, melody to madness, cadence to catastrophe. God lives; it is Nietzsche who is dead.

The wooden cross is no longer characterized by the crashing cymbal of despair, but is rather a rhythmic symbol of hope. It reminds us to strive to keep both crossbeams in perfect tension, the horizontal love relationships between ourselves and others, the vertical faith relationship between ourselves and God. And Jesus is the center where these two become one. Only with both can the cross remain upright. We must be conservative in faith and liberal in love. The cross is *the* symbol of the paradox of life and death:

> *a magnet for human faith and fear.*
> *a nexus point to another world.*
> *a wrinkle in time to eternity.*
> *a drawbridge to the Kingdom of God.*
> *a coda between a symphony of human sorrow*
> *and a symphony of everlasting joy.*

❧

> *I asked Jesus, "How much do you love me?"*
> *"This much." He answered, and He stretched out*
> *His arms and died.*
> ANONYMOUS

Eagles

I bore you up on eagle wings and brought you here to myself.
                                                          Exodus 19:4b

A man found an eagle's egg and put it in the nest of a backyard hen. The eaglet hatched with the brood of chicks and grew up with them. All his life the eagle did what the chickens did, thinking he was a backyard chicken. He scratched the earth for worms and insects. He clucked and cackled. And he would thrash his wings and fly a few feet into the air. Years passed and the eagle grew very old. One day he saw a magnificent bird far above him in the cloudless sky. It glided in graceful majesty among the powerful wind currents, with scarcely a beat of its strong golden wings. The old eagle looked up in awe. "Who's that?" He asked. "That's the eagle, the king of the birds," said his neighbor. "He belongs to the sky. We belong to the earth — we're chickens." So the eagle lived and died a chicken, for that's what he thought he was.
            From Anthony De Mello's *The Song of the Bird*

We were created as eagles. We chose to become chickens. But the majestic Golden Eagle came to us and showed us how to fly. Chickens of earth can now become eagles, and fly throughout the heavens.

Sometime around 30 A.D., an explosion occurred, with a power so awesome that its shock waves are still being felt today — the resurrection of Jesus Christ. Not only did it change the

158

lives of millions, it altered the very fabric of the universe. Just as the splitting of the atom in the 1940's created a massive nuclear fission chain reaction in matter, this event caused a massive reaction in the nuclear family of mankind — the ultimate fusion of God and humanity. Just as the atomic events of the 20th century altered our understanding of physics, the event of the resurrection in the 1st century altered our understanding of metaphysics. With the dawning of hope for new life, humanity now mattered. Because of the resurrection, it is not that "something is now meaningful," but rather that "everything is now infinitely meaningful." Compared to the resurrection of Jesus Christ, the atomic detonation was a mere firecracker. But more important is how they contrast. For the atom bomb created horrendous human suffering and meaningless destruction, but the "adam" bomb (in Hebrew, the word "adama" means "from the ground," *humus* in Latin from which comes the word *human*) of the resurrection has created wondrous human joy and meaningful liberation. Our deepest hope has come true.

A golden eagle, of grace and majesty, is among us.
We can become eagles.
We can learn to fly.

Upon hearing of His arrest, the disciples of Jesus responded in true "chicken" fashion. They hid in fear of their lives. But a short time later, a transformation occurred, and the fearful became fearless. With the valiancy of eagles, they proudly proclaimed that death no longer can harm them, that there is hope for humanity, and we need only to surrender our lives to Christ. What happened to these men and women? What turned them from despairing to daring, from cowards to courageous? There is only one adequate explanation — their explanation. Jesus Christ rose from the dead!

He was not a ghost, not a resuscitated corpse, not a reincarnated spirit, not an enlightened mind, not a vision, not an assumption, not a legend, not a myth, and not a symbolic memorial. Jesus rose from the dead with a glorified body, and He was alive again. The tomb was empty, they had seen Him with their own faithful eyes. And these disciples were willing to put their lives on the line for what they knew to be true. They would now go where only *eagles dare*. Despite this amazing witness from the past, doubts about the validity of the bodily resurrection still linger in the present. Having been "chickens" all our lives, the secure earth is hard to give up. Flying can be dangerous. And perhaps this freedom of flight is too good to be true. Yet when examining the resurrection accounts, a reasonable mind will still point to faith:

Hallucination? How could so many qualified witnesses, including five hundred at one time (1 Cor 15) all have the same hallucination? Besides, hallucinations tend not to eat, get touched, talk, and last for forty days. In John's Gospel, Thomas is invited by the risen Jesus to touch His nail-torn hands.

Conspiracy? Why would the disciples die for a lie? We lie to save our lives, not to lose them. We lie to put ourselves in a *better* position, not a worse one. Usually in a conspiracy, someone will confess the lie? Yet not *one* person ever came forward to explain the forgery. And no one ever produced the corpse, which would have toppled the conspiracy.

Myth? Perhaps the disciples really preached that we should "remember Jesus," and over time this was transformed into the mythological language of a "risen man." No, not enough time. Based on the earliest textual reference to the resurrection, 1 Corinthians 15, we know for a fact that Paul was proclaiming the resurrection in the early 40's, and he was quoting a liturgical formulation that dated even earlier. And the Gospel accounts are too historical to be myth. There are mythological elements to the story, because Christ was the fulfillment of our mythic hopes, but it is clearly written as factual truth. If there had been an earlier proclamation of Jesus merely to be remembered, we would be able to identify elements of that first layer of writing on Christ's death that later mythology built upon, but none of this exists. Besides, 2 Peter 1:16 states very explicitly that the resurrection is *not* a myth.

When we read this early proclamation of the resurrection in 1 Cor 15:3-8 our hope takes flight:

> *I handed on to you first of all what I myself received, that Christ died for our sins in accordance with the Scriptures; that he was buried and, in accordance with the scriptures, rose on the third day; that he was seen by Cephas, then by the Twelve. After that he was seen by five hundred brothers at once, most of whom are still alive, although some have fallen asleep. Next he was seen by James; then by all the apostles. Last of all he was seen by me, as one born out of the normal course.*

The gallant men and women of the early Church offer us a dream that is true. In our sleep, we all have had dreams where we effortlessly fly, only to wake up to our earthbound reality. But this earthbound life *is* but a dream compared to the awakening to eternal life that will take place in the Kingdom of God. The tomb on earth is not the end, our destiny is the skies of heaven. And heaven is not a dream like Peter Pan's Never Land, but rather an *Ever* Land — ever joy in everlasting love. The resurrection of Christ, *the* central fact of human history, bears witness to this truth. We can be eagles and belong to the sky. But first we must go where only eagles dare. Starting as eaglets, we can learn from *the Skymaster* the heights of selfless love, for only the humble can be exalted. He will teach flights of effortless faith, for only the fearful bury their heads in the ground. But before Jesus will carry us, we must rid ourselves of the sinful, self-centered preoccupations of earth — including the fear of death — that weigh us down. They do not belong in the heavens. We can take a tip from the angels, for as G.K. Chesterton reminded us: *"Angels can fly because they take themselves lightly."* Jesus the Golden Eagle will take us to Himself and together we will soar. We need only to surrender the earth, and take to the sky — second star to the right, and straight on until morning.

❧

Think of all the joy you'll find, when you leave the
world behind, and bid your cares goodbye...
you can fly, you can fly, you can fly.

FROM WALT DISNEY'S *PETER PAN*

Santa Claus

For if we believe that Jesus died and rose, God will bring forth with him from the dead those also who have fallen asleep believing in him.   1 Thessalonians 4:14

I believe in Santa Claus.

No, I don't mean a nebulous "spirit of Christmas," nor Santa as a metaphor or a symbol. I mean I believe in Santa Claus. I believe he brings presents every year to little children on Christmas morning. He gave me some great ones. However, I grow more and more concerned over the years, finding adults and teens that don't believe in the big guy. This is tragic because they're not hearing the real truth. There is a Santa Claus! Believe in Santa Claus. In defense of the jolly old saint, here is my argument for the existence of Santa Claus. Read it carefully, the fate of your future Christmases and your children's future Christmases depends on it.

Santa Claus, like any important historical figure, carries a name that has undergone great changes over the years, not unlike the name Jesus, which is probably better translated as "Yeshua" from the Aramaic. So the name Santa Claus is derived from Saint Nicholas. Saint Nicholas lived in the 4th century in Asia Minor. He was Bishop of Myra and was famous for his miracles, piety, and passion for the faith. He suffered imprisonment and was even present at the famous Council of Nicea in 325 A.D. Because he lived so long ago, much of the facts surrounding his life are couched in legend. Legend has it that he secretly gave three bags of gold to a poor father who had three daughters. (As a father of three girls, I can only say, that this is my kind of Bishop!) The gifts helped the family escape poverty. Nicholas died and was buried in Myra. He may have been gone but he was not forgotten. By the Middle Ages, over 400 churches were dedicated to his memory. But this is where the story begins.

Remember, we are Christians. Stop thinking human and start thinking Christian! If we die with Christ we rise with Christ. We can share in the resurrection of Christ. We are *more alive* in heaven, not less! We're not a ghost or a phantom in heaven. And we're not absorbed into a great cosmic "beyond" either. Too many Christians have a Hindu-like concept of heaven, complete with clouds, harps, and winged babies — thinking we are a shadow of ourselves in heaven. This is not only a boring image to some, but, far worse, a misleading image to many. As C.S. Lewis tried to explain, we're in the "shadowlands" now. Heaven is more real, not less real than earth. We are a shadow of our true selves on earth. Lewis wrote about this in *The Great Divorce*, which can baptize our imagination regarding heaven. Lewis described heaven as having a concrete existence, with every blade of grass being like steel. This promise of living a deeper reality in heaven and being a resurrected body has profound implications for each of us, and for the way we view the jolly old saint.

Nicholas is really, truly alive in the Kingdom of God. Upon his death, Nicholas, along with the entire communion of saints, shares in the work of the risen Christ on earth — in a very real way. This is why it is so important to believe. Your faith in Santa Claus is a testimony not to the faith of Christmas, the incarnation, but to the faith of Easter, the resurrection and the communion of saints.

Faith challenges us to think in terms of the invisible as well as the visible. Hebrews 11:1 says that faith is the confident assurance concerning what we hope for, and conviction about things we do not see. It is what we *don't* see that is important. Antoine de Saint-Exupery wrote this in his classic adult fable *The Little Prince*. As the fox reveals to the prince:

It is only with the heart that one can see rightly;
what is essential is invisible to the eye.

Consider this question. After listening to a wonderful music recital, should we respond by complimenting the musician or by complimenting the instrument he played? Surely the instrument is an important part of the music making, but the source of the music is the musician. We would compliment the source — the musician. I doubt we would mistakenly credit a piano for the music, for a piano without a pianist makes no music. We must not make this same mistake with Christmas. If we see a mother buying a Christmas present for her child for Christmas morning, we must not mistakenly credit the mother without recognizing the source of her love. She is the instrument, not the source. The *Source* is Christ along with the communion of saints. And who among the saints is more called upon by the prayers of children at Christmas time than Saint Nicholas? Whether or not he wears a red suit and has a white flowing beard, I cannot say for certain. It is possible. He might. What is important is that we give credit where credit is due. Christ is the source of Christmas love, we are not.

Is this the mere playing of word games? It is not. I am giving a new understanding of Santa Claus. We may want to abandon our childhood *understanding* of Santa Claus, but we should not abandon Santa Claus. Profess our belief in Santa Claus this Christmas and we touch not only the wood of the *manger* in Bethlehem, but also the wood of the *cross* on Calvary.

Even the name Kris Kringle, which we associate with Santa, is derived from the phrase "Dear Christ Child." In other cultures Santa was seen as the messenger from people to Jesus, and it was the Christ child who gave the gifts on Christmas morning. So we see the story of Santa and the story of Jesus are intertwined. Yes, Virginia, there is a Santa Claus. He is alive and well and living in the Kingdom of God. The magic of Christmas in our childhood is replaced by the miracle of Christmas of our second childhood. I truly hope we share this good news about this *Silent Knight* in service to the newborn baby King. If my young child ever looks up at me with doubtful eyes and asks, "Is there really a Santa Claus?" I will smile and look her straight in the eye and say, "Yes, there really is a Santa Claus." It is not a lie. It is the truth. The wonder of Christmas can stay with her, forever childlike in faith. I pray it stay in each of us. This is one gift that can thaw the deepest "winter of our discontent," leaving only the warmth of Christmas love.

Merry Christmas!

*Personally, of course, I believe in Santa Claus;
but it is the season of forgiveness, and I will forgive
others for not doing so.*

G.K. CHESTERTON

Pez

"And you," he said to them, "who do you say that I am?"
"You are the Messiah," Simon Peter answered, "the Son
of the Living God!"   Matthew 16:15-16

The mind loves a challenge. And when it has triumphed, it dismisses the old puzzle and moves on to the next. We like to take a test and be done with it. But the heart remains unsatisfied. For the heart is only content when it is conquered, when it rests in a mystery far greater than itself. A test of the heart is never completed, each day offers continual challenge. And so mind and heart wrestle within us. Some appease the mind and deny the heart, others lead with the heart and ignore the mind. Two parts of our nature are divorced in a sea of conflicts: body and soul, matter and spirit, etc.

We are in need of a marriage counselor. Someone to resolve this divorce that rages inside of us. And so our God, with us for better or for worse, offers us a reconciliation. Eternity steps into time. Jesus Christ is the "marriage moment" — for in Him, God and man, heart and mind, life and death, are in union. All seeming contradictions are resolved in Jesus, the Prince of Paradox.

And the bouquet is thrown to us as well, in hopes of an upcoming marriage. Jesus offers the gift of faith, and faith will take us where reason cannot go by itself. To receive this gift, Jesus does not say to become like an adult. We must become like a *child* to enter the Kingdom and begin the marriage within and

167

heal the "great divorce" that rages in ourselves, our relationships, and our world. We only need to say "I do" and let the children lead.

I was just about finished tucking my five-year-old daughter Clare into her bed. I had completed the mandatory three songs, one drink of water, and one-half chapter from *The Chronicles of Narnia*. I had finally reached my well-deserved "goodnight," when she asked, "Daddy, was Jesus a person or was he God?" Oh, great. What could I tell her that would make sense to a five-year-old? Could I explain that grown-ups for centuries have been battling over the nature of Jesus, that wars had been fought over this question, that Church councils had debated it, that philosophers had spent their lives clarifying this conundrum?

"Both," I said and I reached for a Pez dispenser. Perhaps my trusty Pez would bail me out. "Clare, where would you buy a Pez dispenser? At a candy store or a toy store?"

"A candy store," she decided, but then began to think over that choice. "Maybe a toy store, too."

"So Pez is *both* a toy for play and candy for a treat," I said, "that's pretty much the same with Jesus. He is both God and man at the same time, just as Pez is both a candy and a toy."

"Okay," she said, "I love you Daddy, goodnight."

And our conversation ended, as simply as it had begun. Clare went to sleep, satisfied that although she didn't fully understand my explanation, it was enough to keep her faith in Jesus strong. She nestled into the mystery and found blissful sleep. She looked as content as Pooh after a jarful of honey. As I left her room, I wondered who had been the teacher and who had been the student. I was still holding the Mickey Mouse Pez dispenser. "Not exactly St. Patrick and the shamrock," I thought, "but then again, not bad in a pinch."

My daughter's response contained more wisdom than it might seem. For in a child's heart, simple faith can resolve what a "grown-up's" doubting heart cannot grasp. Adults want all the

168

answers, so we can feel in control. But questions of faith can only be resolved by God being in control. We must accept the fear and transcend it in faith. The trusting heart of a child will show the way.

The heart must always aspire for the trinity of gifts often best exemplified in a child; faith, hope and love. But reason still has an important part to play. Our faith should be reasonable, not blind but bound, and bound to *Someone* real. The mind seeks truth while the heart seeks love. An adult mind can assist our childlike heart; definitely a marriage made in heaven.

This question of Jesus' nature was extremely important in the early Church, for some sought to use their minds to steer their hearts away from Christ, to keep in control. A debate of the mind became camouflage for a conflict of the heart. As early as the 1st century, a group known as Gnostics believed Jesus to be divine but not human. Jesus only "appeared" to be human because, they believed, matter was hostile to spirit. At the other extreme, Arius, a priest of Alexandria around the 3rd century, believed that Jesus was human, but not divine. Nestorius, the bishop of Constantinople in the 5th century, had the schizophrenic idea that Jesus was actually two separate persons, one human and one divine. It's too bad they didn't have Pez back then, it might have helped. Of course, great leaders like St. Athanasius and St. Cyril defended the true nature of Jesus assisted by the Council of Chalcedon (451 A.D.) which helped to put these heresies to rest: Jesus was one person who had two natures, human and divine. But heresies never die, they only can be buried alive, always threatening to return.

Consider the 20th century. On the streets of Chicago, a militant homosexual group called Queer Nation distributed a handout which intimated that Jesus was gay. At St. Louis University, the Women's Studies Department put up a picture of "Christa" showing Jesus as a big-breasted female. One popular book on Jesus tried to argue that Jesus did not die on the cross, but rather that he married Mary Magdalen and had four children.* The film "The Last Temptation of Christ" portrayed Jesus as a doubting confused man who built crosses for the Romans. Some professional scholars in the "Jesus Seminar" deny the bodily resurrection. Mormons believe that Jesus and God are separate persons, both only of flesh and bone. The Jehovah's Witness believes that Jesus is only an immortal spirit creature, subordinate to God.

If we ask a nonbeliever, "Who do you say that Jesus is?" they tend to respond by calling Him a great teacher, wise man, philosopher, or prophet; but certainly not God incarnate. Yet if Jesus was not the Son of God, then He could only be a liar or a lunatic. We forget that Jesus and the early Church proclaimed Jesus as God! Philosophers don't go around claiming to be God, con men do. Wise men don't go around pronouncing their divinity, the insane do. To avoid this "Lord, liar, or lunatic" trilemma, nonbelievers try to divorce the message from the man, but the man is the message. A man's credibility rests not only on his words, but on himself. So if we're ever confused by the distorted images of Jesus around us, we can buy some Pez candy and read our Bible. Jesus is the same: past, "pez-ant," and future: true God and true man.

Apply reason to faith and marital peace can reign within. I admit I don't understand *how* a person can be both human and divine at the same time, but then again, I still don't know how the toaster works. I don't understand the television or usually what's on it, but I can still use it. I don't understand how to properly load a Pez dispenser, but I still can eat the candy. I definitely don't understand women, but I can still have a relationship with my wife. I don't fully understand Jesus' nature, but I still need Him. Life is not a problem to be solved but a mystery to be lived.

---

* Data for this paragraph was taken from *US News* (12/5/94) and *Life* (12/94) magazines.

Living the mystery of Jesus is what I had offered my daughter at bedtime that one night. She will find it more wonderful than any toy ever played with, and sweeter than any candy ever tasted. The interior spiritual struggle, which had always been conflict for us is resolved in Jesus. The war is over, the Prince of Peace reigns. And though His nature will remain a mystery for us, faith resolves what reason cannot fully grasp. The "great divorce," our separation from God and from ourselves has ended in Christ. He is the "marriage moment," the union of:

> *heaven and earth,*
> *heart and mind,*
> *matter and spirit,*
> *body and soul,*
> *service and freedom,*
> *life and death.*

We can only understand when we "stand under" Christ. The confusion ends in Jesus, the Prince of Paradox, the holy fusion of God and man. Enough of our fighting, we have a marriage to celebrate.

❧

You can shut Him up for a fool, you can spit at Him
and kill Him as a demon, or you can fall at
His feet and call Him Lord and God.
But let us not come with any patronizing nonsense
about Him being a great human teacher. He has
not left that open to us. He did not intend to.

C.S. LEWIS

Triple Play

In the beginning was the Word,
and the Word was with God,
and the Word was God.   John 1:1

In baseball, double-play combinations are entertaining and fairly common in an average game. Triple plays are rare. An *unassisted triple play* in a *World Series* seems unfathomable to the average fan. But one such play really was experienced by the fans in 1920, performed by second baseman Bill Wambsganss of the Cleveland Indians. It has been recorded in the Official Encyclopedia of Baseball record book. But a phenomenon as incredible as this requires a little more detailed explanation. I will assume a basic knowledge of baseball. In the fifth game of the World Series against the Brooklyn Dodgers, with no men out, runners on first and second, Wambsganss made a spectacular catch of a line drive shot near second base. Both baseman were off and running on the hit, assuming no one could catch the well-hit ball. Wambsganss caught the ball (out #1), stepped on second base (force out #2) and tagged the bewildered base runner moving toward him from first (out #3). The Indians eventually went on to win the series, and an *unassisted triple play* has never happened in a World Series since.

There is a cosmic *triple play* that seems unfathomable to the average Christian. But one such "play" really was experienced by early Christians of the 1st century. It was recorded in the Bible, God's official record book. The one God is three persons, He exists as an unassisted *triple play*. But a phenomenon as incred-

172

ible as this requires a little more detailed explanation. I will assume a basic knowledge of God and love. God does not express love, God *is* love. So no matter how great we can imagine love to be, God is even greater. But love requires three things: a lover, someone to love, and a love relationship between them. This is true of human nature because it is true of God's nature, since we were made in his image and likeness. So God the Father (person #1) eternally loves God the Son (person #2), and the love relationship between them produces God the Holy Spirit (person #3).

But this *triple play* formula was not invented in the mind of man to be imposed on God; we witnessed this phenomenon in life. Only later did we develop the philosophical words to better explain it. The early disciples were devout Jews who believed in God the Father because they had experienced the miracle of His creation. Then they met Jesus and, because of the miracles of the incarnation and resurrection, they believed Him to be God the Son. Then they experienced the miracle of God the Spirit within themselves at Pentecost. They had experienced the ultimate "triple play."

But this miracle does not live only in the past, we can still encounter the triune God by entering the "game." We must surrender our lives over to the Son. With Christ at our side, we will love the Father, as demonstrated by the Son, and the Spirit of both of them will dwell within us. With the power of God within, we will win the "World Series" and defeat our triple threat opponents: sin, evil and death. In fact, God's team is undefeated.

God wanted for us the joy and peace that is Himself. That is why the Son incarnated Himself and entered our human history, to break through the "cloud of unknowing" that lies between ourselves and an invisible, inaudible, intangible God, and show us the way back to Himself. We were made to be with God. No "pinch hitter," be it drugs, sex, romance, art, or any other, can substitute for God on this team. So to ensure victory, our ultimate Manager became a player-coach, one of us, to teach us how to win. God becoming human would be comparable to a human becoming a larvae. But "sacrifice" is part of His game plan.

Aside from God's major revelation of His nature through Jesus Christ, He has left other "minor league" clues as well in creation. Time is divided into past, present, and future. In chemistry, the single nature of water (H^2O) can take the three forms of ice, liquid, and mist. In geometry, one cube consists of squares in three dimensions — length, width, and depth. In physics, a single atom consists of three interacting particles — proton, neutron, and electron.

There is another very important sign of the Trinity in our world. A few years ago I was giving a talk to a group of eighth-grade students, attempting to explain to them the Trinity. I concluded my explanation by saying, "Now, none of us can understand how the love between the Father and the Son can produce another unique Person, the Spirit." "I think I understand it," said a young girl who was listening.

"Oh really," I responded, "Please, explain it to us." In my mind I seriously doubted that this little girl could make simple what I, a superior educated grown-up could only explain using complicated theology. "A baby," she calmly explained, "a baby is a unique person who is the union of love between a mother and father."

The simple wisdom of the girl left me speechless, and feeling rather ashamed. She had humbled my exalted ego. Yet more importantly, she had revealed an essential truth about humanity and divinity. The human family is a *mirror* that reflects the very nature of God Himself! The human trinity reflects the divine Trinity. The family is not an outmoded human invention that should be replaced with new alternative families, as many say in the modern world. The love between husband and wife that can produce a child is a natural reflection of the supernatural God. God built into humanity a blueprint of His own nature to help us come to know Him. And to ultimately demonstrate how important the human family is, He joined one, incarnating Himself as a baby in the holy family of Mary and Joseph, thus revealing to us that *all* families are holy. Every child should be raised in the permanent love of a father and mother. This is the ideal for which we should strive, for it makes possible the opportunity for a child to grow to accept the permanent love in God. The family is a divine invention, and it is the modern world that is outmoded and needs to be replaced.

As with baseball, the object of life is to go home. God proposes that we assist in His *triple play* nature. Live like the Son and love the Father and the Spirit of both will dwell within. Involving ourselves in the *triple play* of God's very nature will bring us Home, from our human family to the divine family of our Creator. And others, witnessing this phenomenon in us, will want to join the team as well. Victory awaits us; it is time to take our position on the championship team.

❧

God cannot fall in love for the same reason why water can't get wet.

PETER KREEFT

Crossroads

After John's arrest, Jesus appeared in Galilee proclaim-
ing the good news of God: "This is the time of fulfillment.
The reign of God is at hand! Reform your lives and be-
lieve in the gospel!"   Mark 1:14

Will you marry me? These four words can make a person
tremble. The answer to this question will shape both individual's
lives and, perhaps, the lives of countless future generations. Now
for most questions there are three possibilities; "yes, no, or
maybe." But for some questions, such as a marriage proposal,
there are only two. We either are married or are not. We can't
be half-married anymore than we can be half-pregnant. To say
"maybe" is to say "no," for we have not begun the marriage relationship. As long as she says "maybe," he stays unmarried. Silence, evasion, or indecision are other ways of saying "no." Ignore the question and you have answered the question. It is the
same with Christianity. Christianity is not an organization, it is
a marriage, and even in death we do not part. Thomas Aquinas
used this image to describe our faith:

> *By faith the Christian soul enters, as it were, into mar-*
> *riage with God.*

Where the marriage analogy breaks down is that the Christian "marriage" is not a marriage of equals. God is clearly in charge
of the relationship (although so is my wife) and is perfectly faithful. He never forgets an anniversary. Jesus, borrowing from His

176

Jewish tradition, used the symbol of the *Kingdom of God* to describe the "God-human" bond. All of the parables and teachings of Jesus revolve around this image. God is our King whose will is to be done on earth as it is in heaven. If God says "Jump!" we say "How high?" The King's will and the Kingdom's will are one. Jesus' challenge of the Kingdom of God, like a marriage proposal, allows only two choices, "yes" or "no." So choose and choose now. Remember, "maybe" means "no." Jesus, then and now, confronts us with this powerful message. There simply is no middle ground.

> *Either radically reject Him, or radically accept Him.*
> *Either "thy will be done" or "my will be done."*
> *Either let God be King or let yourself be king.*
> *Either good or evil.*
> *Either virtue or vice.*
> *Either Jesus or the Devil.*
> *Either heaven or hell.*
> *Either service in humility or puppet kingship in pride.*

This is *the* choice of infinite importance, of eternal consequence.

I sometimes think that if Jesus came today, we wouldn't crucify Him. We would mock Him, ignore Him, or applaud Him and then continue our comfortable life as if nothing had happened. He would be the subject of a "Saturday Night Live" skit. The massive majority of Americans believe in God and have some religious affiliation. We just *act* like there is no God! Religion is marginalized into a Sunday morning ritual alone. A little "God" is okay, but we remain in control. The idea of surrendering our entire existence over to the will of God sounds too "extreme" for many believers. Religion is seen as an act of conformity. We will submit to a few rules, not totally submit to a Ruler. That's something extremists do. It was said by Archbishop Fulton J. Sheen that if the Soviet Union was "the cross without Christ," America is "Christ without the cross." We ignore the essential faith that Jesus proclaimed, thinking that we are on a compromise middle road. But there is no middle road, only two very distinct roads, and we are at the *crossroads*. We all choose a King. As C.S. Lewis once wrote:

> *There are only two kinds of people in the end: those who say to God, "Thy will be done," and those to whom God says, in the end, "thy will be done."*

Christianity is an act of cultural, political, social, and personal *revolution*! We are called to place King above country, King above family, King above self. God is King and we are not! And the choice we make is the most essential distinction that exists between humans. All other distinctions; black or white, male or female, young or old, rich or poor, capitalist or socialist, etc. these are important but not essential. This is our fundamental option, the proposal of eternal marriage, and the choice will shape our destiny.

Like a surgeon, Jesus attacks the cancerous "false god" inside each of us and offers to remove it. And we resist the surgery because it is painful. I wish I could say that being a Christian is a bed of roses, but there are thorns. G.K. Chesterton understood the Christian "operation":

> *It's not that Christianity has been tried and found wanting, it's that Christianity has been found difficult and therefore not tried.*

The glamour and deceptive nature of sin is always present, attempting to draw our attention away from Christ, trying to get us to place "self in the center" of our existence rather than an invisible God. But we must keep our eyes on the prize, knowing that the center of sin is "I," and renewing ourselves by continually turning back to Him in forgiveness, placing the Creator in the center of creation.

Let's pretend. When I was a kid, there was a game show on TV called *Let's Make a Deal* where people would dress up in goofy outfits and gamble with the host. Towards the end, a contestant could choose to keep their money (let's say $100) or trade it for what's behind Door #1, Door #2, or Door #3. Behind one of those doors was a great prize (let's say $10,000). Behind another was an even trade, and behind another was nothing. The contestant had a 33% chance of winning the great prize. What would you do? Would you hold on to the money or take a chance? What if I told you that the $10,000 was behind Door #1 and my information is reliable, legal and ethical? It's hard to imagine that anyone would prefer to keep the $100 rather than $10,000.

Let's make a deal. God calls us to "make a deal" as well, to trade in our earthly life — it has a limited, finite value anyway — for a chance at *eternal life*! And here's the good news, everyone who makes the deal wins, a 100% return on investment. And if eternal life is not enough for us, God will even sweeten the offer, even better than a set of ginzu steak knives. He will give us *back* our earthly life, better than it was before because now we're on the *Master* plan. God knew what was best for us before we were born. He knows our true destiny. Yet as spectacular as this offer is, we can stubbornly choose to cling to an earthly life that we're going to lose anyway, rather than accepting the ultimate prize from the Ultimate. What a tragedy. We are meant for more. Each of us is unique, a miracle. Each of us is a central piece of the crossword puzzle of life, and unless we assume responsibility for that piece, the puzzle is never completed. Just as Mufasa said to his son Simba in the film, *The Lion King*, so too, God says to us right now:

You are more than what you have become.

Most of us like to take a test and be done with it. But with

Jesus, each day we keep getting tested. Every day is another "amen — let it be so" to God, another self-surrender, until the final exam. Christians must take the test and meet the challenge of the Kingdom. But we need not take it alone. With Jesus on our side, what we saw as a test becomes a proposal, and life becomes a marriage made in heaven. At this very second, we are at the *crossroads* of human existence. Let us choose the cross at the *crossroads*.

❧

The greatest act of faith is when a man decides that he is not God.

OLIVER WENDELL HOLMES, JR.